How to Talk to the "Other Side"

Finding Common Ground in the Time of Coronavirus, Recession & Climate Change

Kevin Wilhelm

Natalie Hoffman

Edited by:

Petra Barbu

Ruth Lee

Katie Secrist

First Printing: 2020

ISBN 978-0-578-67132-1

Kevin Wilhelm
Seattle, WA

www.kevin-wilhelm.com

www.sustainablebizconsulting.com

For Kirby and all of us

Table of Contents

Section 1: Beginning the Conversation

Introduction...3

Finding Common Ground....................................7

Section 2: Coming Together Case Studies

1: Republicans vs. Democrats........................17

2: Rural vs. Urban America..........................29

3: Big Business vs. Environmentalists 43

4: Climate Skeptics vs. Climate Advocates...........61

5: Military vs. Sustainability.......................75

6: Fossil Fuels vs. Renewable Energy................81

Section 3: Communication Tools

The Importance of Allyship........................91

Difficult Conversations 101.......................103

Conclusion...113

How to Start a Conversation in One Page.............115

References...117

How To Read This Book

This book is broken down into 3 distinct sections, clarified below to help the reader:

Section 1: Beginning the Conversation

This section level sets and provides insight into everyday ways to find common ground with people you don't agree with. These are designed to be lighter, less controversial ways to begin the conversation.

Section 2: Coming Together Case Studies

These six chapters are the meat of the book and address some of the most contentious issues in our current US society. Each chapter lays out the disagreements between two adversarial groups, takes a deep dive as to why there is such animosity, and then provides real life win-win examples of ways in which they can come together.

Section 3: Communication Tools

This section is truly about "The How." How do you communicate more effectively? How can we both listen to and be heard by the "other side" and how can we be allies to those most affected by this divisiveness?

Please note that this book is written from the first-person perspective of Kevin Wilhelm, the lead author.

Acknowledgements

Kevin Wilhelm: I'd like to give a special thanks to my team – Petra Barbu, Ruth Lee and Katie Secrist for their help in crafting this book, providing feedback and helping with the final edits. I'd also like to thank them for giving me the time and space to write this book during such a busy time for our company.

I have to thank my co-author Natalie Hoffman for her constant energy, research, editing and ideas. Throughout this entire process you helped us reformulate the narrative, constantly improving it and making the writing process both fun and collaborative, especially as life around us has changed dramatically since we started writing this book.

I'd like to thank my son Kirby, who was part of the inspiration for writing this book. It is my hope that we can return to a time of civility and cultural understanding by the time you read this.

More than anyone though, I'd like to thank the love of my life Jo for her love and for helping keep our family balanced during these ever so challenging times. I love you and without your support, I wouldn't have the courage to take on such an endeavor.

Natalie Hoffman: A big thank you to Petra Barbu, Ruth Lee and Katie Secrist for welcoming me to the team and showing me such genuine kindness. Your input was often exactly what we needed to hear and helped shape this book.

I'd like to send my appreciation to the professors and role models in my life who have been instrumental in giving me direction. Thank you also to everyone at Seaplane, who encouraged me as one of their own and made writing this book even more fun.

To my friends, I can't thank you enough. You always pick me up in my toughest moments and have supported me so positively through this incredible writing process.

I send my sincere gratitude to my co-author Kevin Wilhelm for being so devoted to my development as an individual. You are an impactful mentor, an amazing author and CEO and, most importantly, a wonderful friend.

Finally, and most of all, thank you to my family. I am filled with love and gratitude for your dedication to my happiness and success. I can only write this book with authenticity because you always taught me to be kind, optimistic, compassionate and respectful. You always have, and will continue, to inspire me.

Special thanks to the following interviewees:

The authors would like to thank the following individuals who were interviewed for this book. They provided valuable insights, ideas, moral support and validation for many of the solutions in this book. The conversations with each of you have shaped our thoughts, and we are most grateful.

Benji Backer, Josh Chaitin, Laura Clise, Ericka Dickey-Nelson, Patrick Drum, Peter Fenn, Holly Fretwell, Kevin Hagen, Anne L. Kelly, Natasha Lamb, Ross McFarlane, Bruce McGlenn, Tim Moore, Todd Myers, Steve Nicholas, Ben Packard, Joanie Parsons, Dave Phemister, Sandra Richard, Jason Rodney, Rhys Roth, KoAnn Vikoren Skrzyniarz, Katie Songer, Kim Vu and Letitia Webster

Thank you!

Section 1:

Beginning the Conversation

Introduction

Why we need this book

The Coronavirus pandemic and the resulting economic recession makes this a uniquely challenging time in our country's history. Unfortunately, while we face these great challenges, our country seems to be as polarized as we've been since the Civil War – not just politically, but also culturally and socio-economically.

Tribalism has set in where people choose the facts and news sources they want to believe and increasingly dig their heels into their own camps and belief systems. This self-selecting and mass siloization has resulted in a bubble effect, where people only communicate, socialize with and listen to others who share their same beliefs. They don't want to be associated with people from the "other side," and often avoid interacting with them altogether.

While this would test us during normal times, the current polarization is leading us into dangerous territory. The feeling by many that we no longer share the same values as people from the "other side" is a threat to us as individuals and as a country, especially as we face multiple public health, economic, and environmental crises.

In the lead up to this book, I asked myself – can we get past this divisiveness and return to a time of unity? This question has only been amplified as our daily lives have been disrupted, uprooted, and for many, changed forever in ways that would been unfathomable at the beginning of 2020.

Can we come together as one people to step up and solve these great challenges?

The answer is yes. I believe strongly, just like the Greatest Generation did during World War II, that we not only can, but we must.

This book is about hope, optimism and practicality. It is not about finding ways to "convince" the other side that you are right and that they are wrong, nor is it about trying to get someone to switch political parties or point blame on how Covid-19 should have been handled. Instead, it is about finding common ground not only through small actions, but also through the foundation of our shared aspirations and humanity. If we are going to meet today's challenges, we first have to get back to being able to talk to one another.

Our goal was simple – to provide a beacon of light during these difficult times and illustrate a path forward. Chock full of real-world case studies, we wanted to provide the reader with practical tools and win-win scenarios from countless interviews, conversations and research that will help us achieve the unity that we so desperately need right now.

How did we get to this point?

There was a time not too long ago where we didn't let points of disagreement divide us so drastically and define who we are.

Looking back at my own childhood, I grew up in a small town where everyone identified as Americans first and foremost. Our identities were defined by our tight knit community, where our parents worked and sometimes which religion we followed.

I was raised Episcopalian, but I had friends who were Catholics, Baptists, Presbyterians, Jews, Hindus, Buddhists and Atheists. During election years, people voted by party line but didn't define themselves solely as a Democrat or as a Republican. Nobody said they were from a Red state or Blue state. Politics was just a small part of what defined us, how we viewed the world and how we interacted with others.

All of that has seemed to change in the last dozen years or so. People are increasingly identifying themselves by their political affiliation as some type of quick substitute for their entire belief system. Part of this is due to the rise of social media and the growth of hyper-partisan news sources such as MSNBC and Fox News.[1] Part of it is also a result of gerrymandering.

The majority, however, stems from the micro-geographical segmentation and targeting that our technology now affords us through the internet – including our news, shopping, eating and social media habits.[2] This has not only changed the discourse, but has influenced our ability to trust or even converse with people from the opposite side of the aisle, which is especially important to be able to do during times like these.

Most Americans are just trying to get by. They are overloaded trying to balance work, life, taking care of their families and just don't have enough time in their day. This was been compounded in the Spring of 2020 with sheltering in place and the need to home school their kids. So, when they are so overwhelmed, they just want to escape to their favorite Netflix show, social media feed or news app because it provides a sense of calm, comfort and community. This all contributes to the creation of an echo chamber, where people only turn to the places, people and information that they already agree with and avoid disagreeable conversations.

If this is the case, how can we come together to solve the problems that are facing our country - our public health crisis, our economy, failing school systems and climate change? These are the questions this book works to solve.

"We may not agree on everything, but enough is enough! We have to get back to having conversations with people – no matter who they voted for."

– Tim Moore, Managing Director, Milamber USA[3]

Start with shared aspirations

Something I've uncovered from the numerous interviews, meetings, countless conversations and research that led to this book is that for the most part, we all share the same aspirations. We all want to have a healthy family, a meaningful job, good schools for our kids, a safe community and a vaccine for the Coronavirus!

We can agree on common goals, which I refer to as "the ends."

Disagreement often stems from how to get there, or "the means."

The arguments, divisiveness and toxicity stem from these means. We get stuck in the process of making decisions depending upon our perception of who wins, who loses and our partisan viewpoints. Since we have lost the ability to listen, understand and compromise with the "other side," we've allowed ourselves to get bogged down on these differences instead of focusing on our shared aspirations and working to achieve those.

The reality is that this country is full of good people. We've all shown our willingness to sacrifice for the greater good and make major life changes during the pandemic. It's just that we've allowed the current political environment and media to drive us to a place where we've lost our ability (or even willingness) to be civil in our discourse.

This is especially important during a time of crisis and economic distress. We need to get things done and we need to do so by returning to a time of more tolerance, mutual understanding and respect. Most of us want to get there, too! A 2018 study found that 77% of Americans believe that the differences between Americans are *not* so big that we can't come together, and that was before recent events upended our lives.[4]

We need to move beyond this divisiveness and our own bubbles, because as KoAnn Skrzyniarz, CEO of Sustainable Brands Worldwide says it best, "The stakes are too high, and we will all sink or swim together."[5]

We have more in common with one another than we allow ourselves to believe. We all eat food, drink water, breathe in oxygen and have dreams for the future. When we set our political, ideological or religious views to the side, it's actually quite easy to find common ground with people you don't know or have a difference of opinion with.

Times are tough right now, so the purpose of this chapter is to provide you with a list of ways to build rapport and find camaraderie with someone *before* you try and tackle the bigger, tougher, more divisive conversations found in the meat of this book. Rhys Roth, the Executive Director at the Center for Sustainable Infrastructure (CSI) advises, "Start by listening and framing conversations in ways that don't send people into their ideological bunkers." This is a necessary step and can be done by first connecting on a human or personal level.

Below are some lighter examples I want to highlight where one can have a great conversation, laugh, and share an experience with someone who they might otherwise disagree with on just about every other issue. This can be done by first connecting on topics of comfort and commonality, which I call "The 4 Ways to Level Set a Conversation."

4 WAYS
TO LEVEL SET A CONVERSATION

HOME *Travel*

SPORTS Hobbies & Interests

There are obviously more than four areas of interest to talk about, but I've found that these are especially easy and neutral topics politically, ideologically and generationally which put you on the same level with anyone you are talking to, especially when today's news can feel so heavy.

Home

This is the easiest entry point into any conversation because everyone is from somewhere. If you ask someone to describe where they call "home," this immediately level sets the conversation because no matter your job title or socio-economic status, we are all from somewhere.

I've found this to be true both personally and professionally, as it is a much better conversation starter than asking someone, "What do you do?" When you lead with the latter question, you run the risk of starting off on the wrong foot – especially if they don't like their job, are unemployed or are worried they'll be judged by what they do or where they work. By starting with "Where are you from?" you level the playing field because there is no "right" answer.

Moreover, when asked what it was like to grow up where they did, people often reminisce about something good or bad about their childhood that allows for deeper conversation. For example, since I grew up in rural Ohio, I can easily relate to other people from Ohio, rural America or even the Midwest. Anyone with experience from those areas understands my roots and I understand theirs, and we can quickly form a bond.

Travel

Travel is also a great unifier – both when you are traveling and when you return home.

Anonymity and commonality while traveling

One of the great things about traveling is that it provides a certain sense of anonymity and enables you to shed whatever ideologies and differences you may have with people.

The other thing that really jumps out at me is the shared commonality that you uncover through travel. Whether it's through conversations with locals or people I run into along the way: I've found that pretty much everyone wants the same thing for their children. No matter the culture, country, language or socio-economic circumstance, every parent shares what I call the "4 Kid Commonalities." They want their children to:

- Be safe

- Grow up healthy + happy

- Get a good education

- Have better opportunities than they had

These are shared aspirations from parents across the globe and are an easy way to find common ground.

When you come home from your travels

Another way travel establishes common ground is, ironically, upon returning home. If an acquaintance or business colleague mentions that they just came back from a trip or vacation, I always ask about it because that is when they are most eager to talk about their travels. It is a great opportunity for connection and a way to level set through the amazing spots you visited, foods you tasted or even travel headaches – whether it's traveling abroad, or visiting Yellowstone, the Mall of America, the Grand Canyon, "The Horseshoe," or Disneyland. Just the fact that you've visited the same place establishes a kind of kinship, where you can easily relate to one another's experiences. Even if you've had a trip cancelled or postponed recently, just mentioning this experience can be a good conversation starter.

Sports

Sports is another great equalizer and connector. When you are at a sporting event, the person sitting next to you may vote differently or hold a totally different value system than you, but during the game you are linked together like brothers and sisters because you are rooting for the same team.

I highlight this because every fan has a personal story behind their fandom. They all have a special moment or reason as to why they support the teams they do – one that filled them with joy and led them to become a fan. And more likely than not, they can share stories of heartache and being let down. That's the nature of sports, and every fan you start a conversation with has a story to share or something to harp about with their current team, management or disappointment in recent season cancellations.

I've found that it's a very rare day that I can't find commonality or conversation with someone about sports. The best part about sports is that it has a unique power of bringing people together from different races, ethnicities, backgrounds, political parties and belief systems.

For example, a few years ago, I was sitting on a panel about climate change in Bellevue, Washington and one of the other panelists and I were put there to kind of "fight it out" on the issue. But before the event officially kicked off, I noticed that the other panelist was live streaming a Seattle Mariners baseball game on his phone. The M's were up by one run in the 9th inning but the other team had two runners in scoring position. He was obviously stressed, so I broke the ice by saying, "Let's hope the bullpen doesn't blow it again tonight." He replied, "I know, right!" This simple act led to a conversation about us being season ticket holders of various teams.

This allowed us to build rapport, which became our foundation while taking part in the panel. Even though we connected on something as meaningless as the Mariners not blowing another lead, this shared passion and pain enabled us to talk civilly with one another and to look for practical climate solutions that found common ground. That's the power of sports.

Sports across cultures

When my wife and I were traveling in Dehradun, India, we rolled into a bus terminal late at night and were stranded there for a few hours with about a dozen locals. I didn't know any Hindi and they didn't speak English, but I did know the name of India's most famous cricketer at the time – Sachin Tendulkar. So, I made eye contact with a few of them and just said "Tendulkar?" They all lit up and one of them said, "Ah, you know Tendulkar" and invited us over to share tea together. Seriously, my wife and I didn't have anything else to offer in Hindi, but that very simple sports connection brought us into their circle.

If you can connect on sports, you can find commonality on more important issues as well.

Hobbies and interests

This last category is intentionally broad because what people do with their free time is incredibly varied. Hobbies are done by choice, fueled by passion and positivity, and they are the very things that people turn to in good times and bad. Therefore, getting to know someone by what hobbies they love opens up all types of doors in conversation and is a great way to level set across different generations. This has been increasingly important recently as people who've been forced to social distance and "shelter-in-place" have had to turn to their hobbies for comfort and find new ways to share their passions online. For many, this was a way of staying positive and keeping a connection during challenging times

I want to take this section's example a different direction though, because I want to highlight the way in which I used a shared hobby to connect with someone from the "other side" who was intent on pissing me off.

A few years ago, I was tabling at an event outside of Olympia, WA as a loaned executive to an environmental nonprofit when a rather burly man came up to me and said, "I like to plow through wetlands, how does that make you feel?" In that moment, I wasn't sure how to respond. There was a part of me that wanted to say, "Who the heck brags about that?" but instead, I took a different approach. I looked at his overalls which were labeled "WA State Dept. of Transportation" and realized that his job was to build roads. He probably saw wetlands as a major inconvenience for his primary job and something that just got in his way. As I searched for more clues, I noticed that he had a Ducks Unlimited patch on his sleeve, and I saw an opening.

I asked him, "Are you a hunter?" He said yes. I asked him where he liked to hunt. And he told me that he grew up hunting elk near Wenatchee, which is in central Washington State. Then I said, "I'm from Ohio originally and they usually hunt deer back home. How is the hunting out here?" To which he responded, "It's certainly not like it used to be, there are all these suburbanites out here with their new housing subdivisions in areas which used to be nothing but wilderness." He stopped mid-sentence because suddenly, he realized that the roads he was plowing were indirectly leading to the loss of his beloved hunting habitat.

He was expecting me to pick an argument, but instead I offered him a conversation about hunting, and it became a bonding moment. I didn't need to say anything more because despite our differences, we both understood that we cared about the exact same things.

Summary

The examples above and in the following chapters are illustrative in helping you level set a conversation with someone from the "other side," because we all have things in common. Use the 4 Ways to Level Set a Conversation as entry points (or one of your own - food, music, dogs, etc.) to get the conversation started and you'll be surprised about what can follow.

When talking with someone you perceive to be on the "other side" that has different opinions and values from you, an important first step is to listen for shared interests. To do this:

- Start with the non-controversial stuff first

- Ask where someone is from – we're all from somewhere

- Realize common ground exists through sports, travel and hobbies

- Tell stories and laugh about memorable moments

- Connect on a human level

Section 2:

Coming Together

Case Studies

1: Republicans vs. Democrats

We are at an incredibly polarized time in our nation's history. As recently as 10 years ago, politics was just one way in which people identified themselves. Nowadays it seems like it has become *the primary way* in which people view the world, judge others, and the news stories they are going to believe. This hyper-partisanship is even showing up in how our country deals with societal threats such as the Coronavirus and its impacts on people and the economy, as well as longer-term threats such as climate change.

To many, a person's voting pattern – whether they voted for a Democrat or Republican – has become a short-hand stereotype for their moral character and value system. This way of thinking is far too simplified. In reality, the platform of our political party does not define our entire personality, but we've allowed social media to persuade us into having that perception – both in the way we view ourselves and how we judge others.

An individual's political preference often has more to do with the result of their personal experiences, hopes, fears and upbringing. Neither Democrats nor Republicans uniformly support every position or statement their party/candidate makes. There is common ground to be had, especially as we think about our response to the pandemic, the recession and how we recover as a country.

While we remain polarized, there has been a hint of coming together led by regular Americans. During the Coronavirus pandemic, the majority of individuals and communities (no matter their political party) have been sharing in the sacrifice of sheltering in place to protect our most vulnerable and for the benefit of all, even as our news outlets continue to offer up partisan talking points.

Another more mundane example from the more normal times of 2019, was when Van Jones (a liberal political commentator) and the Koch brothers (major Republican donors) demonstrated an ability to come together and work towards successful criminal justice reform. They did this even though they despise each other's stances on almost everything else. Common ground can be had because as political consultant Peter Fenn is fond of saying, "We don't have to agree on everything to agree on one important thing!"[6]

In this chapter, I will offer insights into the underlying anxieties of both sides, describe what led to this political polarization and provide case studies of where Republicans and Democrats can come together. I also want to state that while these next few pages touch on our immediate crises, they aren't the sole focus of this chapter or book, since our political divisions existed beforehand and will be with us long beyond these next few months and years.

Segmentation

As I touched on this in the introduction to this book, social and mass media have enabled all of us to become self-selective of our news sources, information and even our friends. Technological algorithms have made this possible through micro-targeting and segmentation. As a result, people are more dug into their camps than they have been in previous election cycles.[7]

"Part of divide is the lack of accountability created by social media," says Letitia Webster, Chief Sustainability Officer of Mission Makers. As a result, "everyone talks to their own echo chamber."

It's important to note that each side ends up having a different orientation of the world – through their own lenses. Even during a pandemic, people were seeing both the problems and solutions through their partisan perspectives. This affected their judgment, reactions and beliefs as to how serious a public health crisis this was at the beginning, how much we should sacrifice for the economy, what actions should be taken and what both the public health and economic solutions should be.

Quite simply, we are at a time where Republicans and Democrats have lost the ability to agree with each other on even simple, common-sense issues.

We have to stop name calling and stereotyping

Stereotyping, which may provide you with some comfort and put your mind at ease, is rooted in laziness. Generalizing and judging an entire group over a single aspect of their identity lacks effort and is not a true attempt to understand the nuanced perspectives of each individual. People stereotype because it's much easier to simply decide, "I like you" or "I don't like you," depending on if you vote R or D, than it is to explore the depth of the lifelong personal experiences that led to their belief system and how they view the world.

The table on the following pages shows traditional stereotyped generalizations for each political affiliation. Though you may agree with many statements on your side, it is also likely that there will be something you disagree with.

Republican/Conservative	Democrat/Progressive
Pro-life	Pro-choice
Pro-business. Want minimal taxes	Pro-workers. Believe higher taxes are needed on the wealthy and big business
The cure to Covid-19 must not be worse than the virus itself	If we don't temporarily shut down and hurry to stop the spread, the economic pain will be much worse
Socially conservative, traditional, isolationist	Socially progressive, more accepting of diversity
Skeptical of scientists	Trust scientists
Anti-immigration. We don't want open borders	Pro-immigrant rights. We are all immigrants

Anti-government. We need less regulation because the free market is better at solving problems than the government	Pro-government. We need it to take care of the less fortunate. Corporations need to be regulated and cannot be trusted. They only work in their own economic self interest
Anti-environment, climate change skeptic	Pro-environment, climate change advocate
Gun rights advocates	Gun control advocates
Religious	Atheist
Anti-labor unions	Pro-labor
Freedom = individualism	Freedom = equal + equitable opportunity
Respect authority, prefer law & order	Distrustful of authority and the police
Surprising + fun research findings[8]	
Food: prefer meat and potatoes	Food: prefer ethnic foods
Dogs: prefer purebreds	Dogs: prefer mixed breeds
View: other countries are big threats	View: other countries are not especially threatening

As you read down these lists, I'm sure your eyes probably first went to the political party you typically vote for. You also probably found something that you questioned or didn't agree with. That is the point. Stereotypes are generalizations of a group that hold some superficial truth but are often a gross oversimplification of an entire population. No one person fits every stereotype that they are faced with, or checks every box associated with their political party.

In fact, I personally know multiple pro-choice Republicans who took the Coronavirus seriously, are proud of their immigrant past, believe in a social safety net and love nothing more than a good meal at an ethnic restaurant. I know plenty of church-going Democrats that work for big business and have full respect for police authority. Of course, it's not always this straightforward, but each side might be surprised at their similarities if they took the time to discover them.

Benji Backer, the President & Founder of the American Conservation Coalition points this out in his interactions with Democrats that, "When I say I'm a conservative environmentalist, it totally changes the culture of the conversation, because people aren't typically expecting Republicans to have the same shared values on the other side of the political spectrum."[9]

Before I outline the path towards agreement, it's important to first recognize why we tend to get stuck. Too often, we get caught up trying to "win" the argument and "convince" the person from the other political party, rather than hearing what they are saying. Instead of genuinely listening while they speak, we are just forming counter arguments in our head. I'm sure we're all guilty of this and we've all experienced how unsuccessful this is in changing that person's mind. Like I said in the intro, we need to shed this mindset.

Communication isn't about going after your harshest critics and trying to convert them to your side.[10] If we want to find mutual understanding between Republicans and Democrats, we first need to peel back the onion a few layers, truly grasp what is fueling their beliefs and then look for commonalities.

Focus on what we have in common

You might hear "I don't trust them," or "We have nothing in common!" This is a sentiment that could come from either side of the political aisle, especially when you look at the polarizing political descriptors at the beginning of this chapter.

This is simply not true. Think back to the last time you went to the grocery store or attended your child's soccer game. Most likely, politics didn't even come up in casual conversation. That is because conversations naturally flow towards mutual points of interest – like the daily work/life struggles that we are all facing in these crazy times we're living in. That's why we should focus on commonalities first.

If we realize that we all just want healthy and happy families, access to good jobs, enough food to fill our bellies and a safe community, then it becomes much harder to demonize the "other side." By first acknowledging our common humanity, we set the conditions for collectively overcoming the challenges in front of us. For example, at the onset of the Coronavirus, there was a lot of partisan finger-pointing and blame, but when each side began to realize that this virus was non-discriminatory and that they all shared the commonality of not wanting their parents and loved ones to die from the virus, it became easier to work together.

What got both sides tripped up, again was "the means." Both sides wanted to stop the virus from spreading and destroying the economy (and cynically their election chances) which was "the ends," but they were getting tripped up by how best to do it.

Even during more normal times, people allowed themselves to get tripped up on "the means." Let's use the example of guns. Neither Republicans nor Democrats want to see more mass shootings in schools. However, we often get bogged down politically because one side sees the solution as greater access to firearms to stop a shooter, while the other is advocating for stricter gun control laws so that a shooter can't get access to one in the first place.

I liken it to religion. For the most part, each religion is trying to guide you on a path to a better afterlife. The differences lie in how you get there – whether you are a Catholic, Hindu, Buddhist, Muslim or other. You typically can't convince someone to switch their religion with facts or data.

We need to come back to these foundations and realize that we all have commonalities, no matter one's political affiliation. Letitia Webster underscores this importance, because "at the end of the day, we all have common values in that we want a bright and thriving future for our children as well as ourselves."[11]

Keys to setting up the conversation

Success in bridging the gap with the "other side" sometimes lies less in *what* is said than *how* it is said – as the tone and format matter as well. This is especially true when trying to get past partisan differences, because you need to create a positive atmosphere in which peaceful and productive conversations can happen.

When I interviewed KoAnn Skrzyniarz of Sustainable Brands, a group that sets up hundreds of conferences throughout the globe with people from across the political spectrum, she reiterated that if you are going to have people with opposing political views on the same stage, you have to set it up fairly so that both sides will be able to participate without feeling attacked. Her advice:

1. Set the rules of the game/conversation and live by them

2. Acknowledge the other person's reality. Everyone has a right to their point of view

3. Be respectful

4. Celebrate progress wherever it is found

5. Talk about shared ambition and things you have in common

6. If you want them to be open, you need to demonstrate being open-minded first

7. Instead of "either/or" thinking, focus on the power of "both/ and"[12]

Remember that it's important to disagree without being disrespectful. For no matter how strong your beliefs, rejecting, insulting and dismissing somebody just because of who they voted for is not productive. While it may be tough to allow them space to express their viewpoint, at the very least give them a chance. Don't name-call and don't let their political party define them in your head. Regardless if you love President Trump or hate him, remember that your character can be just as defined by showing patience and kindness as it can be by your political affiliation.

Money is the great non-partisan equalizer

In my work as a consultant, I'm often amazed at how often people will get animated when we talk about issues like the environment – as they default to the R or D talking points.

However, when we start discussing how to save money through better environmental practices like reducing energy, water or waste, nobody in either political party really has a problem with that. Natasha Lamb, the Managing Partner and Co-Founder of Arjuna Capital echoes this sentiment when talking politics, stating that "money is an equalizing language because it's void of ideology and both parties speak and can understand the language of money."[13] I detail this more in the Big Business vs. Environmentalists Chapter later on.

Ideology melts away when we get back to the basics

"We need to bring ourselves back to seeing each other at the most basic human level instead of through political ideologies," says Bruce McGlenn of Human Nature Hunting.[14]

His group brings people of different political persuasions together to do just that by reconnecting with nature. He is a firm believer that when we get back to the most fundamental aspects of our lives – food, nature and the reason for being – that we realize how similar we are, and our political views and the polarization just melts away.

Summary

We are incredibly divided as a country politically. Both sides seem more content on winning the argument than they do about solving the real-world problems in front of us. Americans increasingly choose the facts they want to believe, the news outlets they want to watch/listen to and the social media they participate in. It is no wonder that Republicans and Democrats struggle to talk to one another!

Therefore, to find common ground Skrzyniarz points out that, "the fundamental difference between Republicans and Democrats isn't about core values, it's about how those values are represented."[15] Understanding this allows us to realize that our political opponents are often oriented to the world differently.

Rather than trying to convince the "other side" to agree with you, we first need to empathize and list to them to truly understand where they are coming from in their hopes, fears and day-to-day reality.

No matter one's political views, we all have pretty much the same shared aspirations of being healthy, happy, having a good job, good schools and opportunities for our kids, and safe communities.

Let's start there. Let's remember that politics is just one small part of who we are, We need to stop getting bogged down in "the means" and our differences for how we want to solve problems, and instead work collectively towards a more positive vision for the world we want to achieve.

To begin, we must:

- Acknowledge that stereotypes, while convenient to label someone, don't actually tell you anything about the person sitting across from you

- Start by focusing on similarities – even those on the extreme right and left have similar personal goals and aspirations

- Realize that we all share the most basic needs

- Understand that we don't have to agree on everything in order to agree on one thing or have a civil conversation with an acquaintance

- Realize the difference between disagreeing and being disagreeable[16]

- Recognize that both sides vote for their own economic self-interest, but for different reasons

- Talk dollars and cents, and the politics will melt away

- Remember that the environment is not just a Democratic issue, just like how religion is not solely a Republican one

Helpful Responses

Comments	Response
(Democrat) You don't care about... / All you care about is...	(Republican) Just because I have different priorities and a different approach to solving problems doesn't mean that I don't care about public health, the environment, our schools, etc.
(Republican) I hate taxes	(Democrat) Everyone hates paying taxes, especially the process of filling out the damn forms! For a lot of people, it's about a feeling of unfairness, that their money is being wasted or that other people are getting a free ride. On the other hand, I usually support funding for road improvements, better hospitals and anything to reduce traffic, what about you?
I care about jobs and the economy	We all do. Some of these great nonpartisan solutions are economic win-wins no matter your political party
(Republican) I don't want immigrants taking American jobs	(Democrat) Are you worried about your own job, or that of someone you know personally? What is your family lineage? Many of our grandparents or great-grandparents came from other countries
(Democrat) I am just so put-off by the language our President uses	(Republican) Though I don't agree with everything he says or does, let me tell you how his policies have made my life easier

2: Rural vs. Urban America

Strong resentment is growing between rural and urban Americans. This resentment exists for many reasons, but mostly stems from the fact that both sides don't think the other understands them, respects them or shares their values. While these opinions are both perceived and real, this chapter explores some of the underlying reasons for these feelings and reveals ways to find common ground between this geographic and emotional divide.

I grew up in a small town in rural Ohio and now live in the urban metropolis of Seattle, so I've experienced these resentments on both sides first-hand. I understand the misgivings each side has and also know that there is more that unites us than divides us.

Therefore, when the Coronavirus started out in urban centers before eventually hitting rural America and stalling the economy, it went from being seen as a coastal/city problem to something that affected all of us. Both sides began to realize that we are all in this together. We need to build off of this to get past the perspectives that both sides have for each other.

The narrative you can expect from both sides

There is a common perception that the two groups choose different lifestyles and are different in terms of what issues they prioritize in life and at the ballot box.[17] Below are some examples of the narratives from each side.

A frequent sentiment from my research and interviews with rural Americans is that they feel like their issues and value systems are *just different* than urbanites. They feel underappreciated, overlooked and looked down upon to the point of outright resentment toward urbanites.

Some memorable phrases I've heard during my interviews include:

- "They have no idea what our lives are like"

- "They don't know where their food actually comes from"

- "Can't they just leave us alone?"

- "Guns are a way of life out here. They're not only for hunting and protection, but are valuable tools in these parts. Why are they always trying to take them away?"

Urbanites feel misunderstood too – they don't like being lumped into one big catch-all category either. Portrayed in the media as "coastal elites," urbanite beliefs on issues like the environment, immigration, gun control, religion and voting patterns merit just as much respect as those of rural America. Their daily experiences are also different. Or as the Coronavirus proved, sometimes issues may just take more time to reach them than they do in densely populated areas.

Some phrases I've heard include:

- "Why don't rural voters recognize that they vote against their own economic self-interest?"

- "The problems of the inner-city are very different than rural America"

- "We live close together, so social distancing is both necessary and very difficult to do"

- "We are afraid of guns because of all the mass shootings that happen"

- "We provide the tax base that subsidizes so many of these rural communities and counties"

This disconnect was further proven in a recent survey by the Pew Research Center, which found that about two-thirds of *both* urban and rural populations said that people in the opposite type of community don't understand the problems they face.[18]

Understanding rural Americans

Nobody likes being told what to do or being talked down to. Rural Americans don't appreciate urbanites telling them what they should care about – especially when it comes to the environment. Farmers and ranchers are the ones living on the land and are in nature every day, rather than being just weekend enthusiasts who recreate, post on social media and then retreat to their homes in the city.

While many urbanites may think of themselves as environmentalists by writing checks and advocating for environmental causes, every day is Earth Day for farmers. They are the ones on the ground, putting their hands into the soil, keeping track of the weather and making sure their plants have the nutrients they need. Their livelihoods are the ones most intimately affected by changes in climate patterns and extreme weather events.

Hunters also feel misunderstood. They resent being treated as 'animal killers' just because they are the ones that pull the trigger. The reality is that hunters are actually far more in tune with nature and animals than many city-goers, for whom tearing off the plastic wrap is the extent of having to work for their meat.[19]

Many hunters are sure to use every last piece of the animal they have just killed for food or otherwise, whereas food waste is most prominent in cities. Lastly, many environmental protections across the US are funded by revenue from hunting and fishing permits.[20]

Some urbanites also tend to stereotype farmers, ranchers and hunters (especially those who speak with a drawl) as less informed and educated – particularly when it comes to science. The reality is that farmers are actually the original scientists. They are constantly using innovative growing, planting, irrigation and pest management techniques, oftentimes saving a portion of their land to run controlled experiments to see what works best. In fact, many of the farmers I know are on the cutting edge of technology – using their smart phones to monitor an individual plant's water needs and delivering it when the plan craves it most.

Taking technology a step further, ranchers no longer go to the stock auction to buy the biggest steer to mate and grow their herd. For animal husbandry, they now go on the internet to match the sperm and eggs to the exact specifications of their animals and order them online. These are sophisticated examples of science and technology that rural Americans use, which demonstrate why they do not like to be stereotyped by city-dwellers as "simpletons" or "country bumpkins."

Understanding urbanites

Alternatively, life in the city is fast-paced and complicated. Depending on one's job, staring at a computer screen and sitting in traffic can consume most of an urbanite's waking hours. Every day, they run into strangers with different social and ethnic backgrounds/experiences, so their views, priorities and solutions are different.

Public health and environmental issues tend to be more in-your-face in cities as well due to high population density. This is especially true when it comes to viruses, trash and pollution, which motivates a more intense urgency for action on these issues. Similar to how urbanite desires for gun control are more tied to safety/crime than it is to hunting/way of life, urbanite viewpoints are strongly influenced by their daily lives.

Just as rural Americans want urbanites to understand and empathize with their issues, urbanites want their opinions and experiences validated, too. Acknowledging their individual experiences and what they care about is essential. Then, personalizing solutions to each side's concerns is one of the most effective ways to resolve topics of disagreement.

Voting against your own self-interest

'Why do they always vote against their own self-interest?'

This is a consistent refrain that urbanites throw out towards rural Americans, often believing that rural Americans allow themselves to be swayed by socially divisive issues that negatively impact their own financial wellbeing.

This hypocrisy is often lost on urbanites, because they too vote against their own economic self-interest by voting to raise taxes. The difference is simply *how* each side defines the term "self-interest."

Rural Americans tend to take it more literally and short-term, viewing taxes from a personal perspective as something that takes money out of their own pocket. The urban angle is often a longer-term "commons" approach, in which people believe their quality of life will improve by paying a little more towards collective long-term investments such as infrastructure, mass transit or addressing homelessness – things that have a greater impact on urbanites.

The reality is that both sides act and vote against their own economic self-interest. It is all based on that individual's perspective. One views the government as the problem, while the others sees it as the solution. Both opinions have merit and the only way to move the conversation forward is to acknowledge and understand how issues affect them personally.

Where common ground exists

The aforementioned study by the Pew Research Institute found that urban and rural residents actually have a surprising amount in common. Both stated that they felt attached to their communities, neighbors and value being near their families. In fact, they found rural and urban residents to be "nearly identical in their concerns about access to hospitals, economic insecurity and job protection" before the pandemic and economic downturn, and we're sure they have only grown more similar since March of 2020.[21] No one wants their tax dollars wasted, no matter where they came from or which "side" they are on and here are some other areas of the study where their levels of concern were similar:

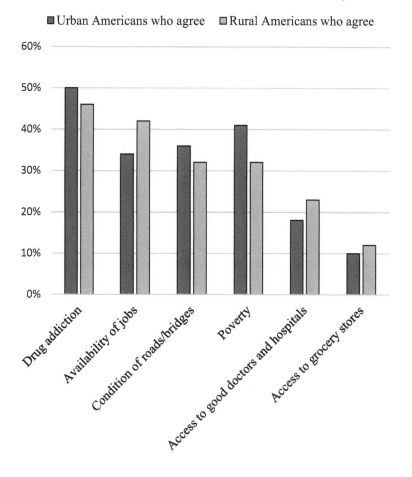

Significant problem in local community:

■ Urban Americans who agree   ■ Rural Americans who agree

Working to resolve the issues listed above provides fertile ground for finding win-win solutions that benefit rural *and* urban Americans. For example, at the onset of Coronavirus outbreak it was viewed primarily as an urban problem because that's where the highest concentration of initial cases were. Many in rural areas felt that "it won't come here." However, eventually, rural Americans felt the exact same anxiety about the virus and needed equal access to testing, doctors and medical equipment, because sickness didn't discriminate towards one group or another.

Win-win solutions

The following five win-win scenarios focus on the most common point of contention between these two groups: helping rural Americans maintain their way of life while enabling urbanites to achieve their environmental goals. Please note that none of these examples have a specific tie to public health, but the economic and environmental benefits can be extremely valuable during these uncertain times where societal and economic norms are challenged.

Turning predators into financial assets

One point of discontent for rural Americans is that they believe urbanites "care more about saving spotted owls and polar bears than they do people!" This resentment is real, and who can blame them?

Rural Americans believe in conserving the natural environment, they just don't want to carry the entire financial and environmental burden of species protection. Ranchers and farmers are the ones who pay the price when a wolf, bear or cougar kills their livestock, uses a wildlife corridor or tramples their crops. They also have to deal with the headache and bureaucracy of trying to get financial reimbursements from the government.[22] Rural Americans are not anti-wildlife – they just want to be treated fairly.

One innovative way of doing this is by following the example of what the American Prairie Reserve (APR) has piloted in Montana. This group has brought together diverse stakeholders to make sure that ranchers and farmers actually benefit financially from the environmental efforts to improve wildlife corridors for bears, wolves and mountain lions.

In the past, if one of these predators killed livestock or trampled their property, the farmers/ranchers had to prove harm to get financial reimbursement from the government – frequently a slow, painstaking, bureaucratic process.

The APR came up with a completely different model. It piloted an innovative solution where it set up motion sensor cameras on participating ranches, and if a bear, wolf or mountain lion showed up on camera, the rancher immediately received a check. They didn't have the red tape of having to demonstrate harm to get reimbursed. They were simply paid any time one of these species traveled across their land.

This changed the mindset for these ranchers, as Todd Myers, the Director of the Center for the Environment at Washington Policy Center described, "from thinking of these animals as a nuisance and a financial liability, to seeing them now as an asset, not only for the environment but for their pocketbooks."[23] This led to an increase in the preservation of wildlife corridors for threatened species that many urbanite environmentalists cared about and was a win-win for everyone involved. This is the type of program that can be replicated across the country.

Finding middle ground in Kentucky

The Kentucky Chapter of The Nature Conservancy (TNC) found a way to address a controversial environmental issue and turn it into a win-win solution for the local economy while honoring the culture of the community.

A dam in the old Kentucky canal system had outlived its usefulness of generating power and failed to do its job of controlling floods and supporting navigation. It had also become a dangerous safety hazard with the threat of collapsing.

The government wanted to remove it to reduce risk to the community, and environmentalists wanted it removed to improve river habitat for species recovery. Community members were against the dam's removal, however, because many held deep-rooted historical and family ties to the dam and the canal, even though it was no longer operational. They preferred the idea of fixing it up over removal.

Previous environmental groups had tried to convince locals and present themselves as the ones with the "right" ideas without actually listening to the community first. Not surprisingly, their efforts failed. Therefore, TNC took a different approach and held a serious of deep listening sessions for community members to vocalize their thoughts and opinions.

In concert with both local and national organizations including the US Army Corps of Engineers, TNC came up with solutions that honored the community's nostalgia and legacy while benefitting them environmentally as well as economically. Rather than ignoring their emotional ties, they brainstormed ways to immortalize the local legacies and history associated with the dam with a display, plaque and educational materials.[24]

Ultimately, the community supported its removal and the state no longer had to worry about the dam failing or catastrophic flooding. The water quality in the canal improved, which helped many local endangered aquatic species return. Recreationalists also began coming to the canal in droves, bringing jobs and money to the community that led to economic development.[25]

Getting to the core of the community disagreement – preserving the community's legacy versus the physical dam itself – allowed positive solutions to arise.

Renewable energy to support the family farm

Many farmers are struggling financially and want more economic stability in their lives. They just want to farm and make a decent living, but they've had a multitude of issues impacting them recently. These include higher production costs, lower commodity prices, the economic downturn, tariffs and extreme weather such as increased droughts and floods.[26]

One solution that many smaller farmers are turning to make up up for lost income is by converting and leasing portions of their land for wind or solar energy. In fact, the average landowner can get paid up to $7,000 -$10,000 annually per turbine or $55 an acre, depending upon the utility rates in their district.[27] Yes, they have to divert a small portion of the land from farming, but this is a viable solution for a family farmer who is surviving on the margins. This is especially needed recently as corn valuations dropped to about $2.70 a bushel with production costs close to $4.20 at the end of 2019.[28] The extra income from these renewable energy projects can help farmers survive the massive economic and price fluctuations listed above that are often out of farmers' control.

"The wind turbine allowed us to be able to keep our family farm," said Jason Wilson from Calhan, Colorado. "It balanced financial viability with sentimental value, allowing the family farm to continue to be passed on to the next generation." This is especially important because according to the American Wind Energy Association (AWEA), about 70% of wind farms in the United States are located in low-income rural counties.[29]

Turning poop into gold

Every problem has a solution. Below are the desires of two groups, which seem divergent in their needs but can actually be aligned:

Rural dairy farmers	Urban climate advocates
Want to avoid government regulations and fines from manure runoff into their drainage ditches	Looking for new renewable energy sources that also reduce greenhouse gas emission

My colleague Kevin Moss, who lived and worked in Mt. Vernon, Washington, had friends who were dairy farmers. They were feeling the pinch of both government and environmental regulation, mostly due to potential fines from the runoff of the cow manure into their drainage ditches and were looking for a solution to this problem.

Enter Farm Power, the company that Moss co-founded, with a win-win solution. They created a process to collect manure from the farmers and use an anaerobic digester to convert the manure and methane into natural gas. At the same time, the local utility was looking for sources of alternative energy to meet the state mandated renewable energy standard and was willing to pay a premium for it.

On top of that, Farm Power generated Renewable Energy Credits (RECs) that were sold to a national retailer that needed these to meet its climate goals. This helped four different stakeholders meet their needs with a solution that was both economically and environmentally beneficial. This scenario literally turned poop into gold.

POSITIVE OUTCOMES

Rural dairy farmers	Urban climate advocates
Lowered environmental remediation costs and potential fines	GHG emissions were reduced by producing renewable energy for the utility
Utility	Retailer
Received new source of renewable energy for distribution	Able to purchase local RECs

Money through conservation

For the rural landowner who wants a stable income and retirement without having to sell their land to a housing developer; conservation easements can be an effective solution. An easement is a long-term voluntary restriction on a property that offers permanent protection for wildlife habitat and provides a lump sum payment and tax advantages for the landowner.

May Ranch in Colorado is a solid example of this. The May family wanted to maintain its 16,000-acre grassland rather than be forced to develop it due to financial pressures. They partnered with several organizations including The Conservation Fund and Ducks Unlimited to place a conservation easement on 90% of the property, which was a key migration corridor for many rare bird species.[30]

To take it one step further, the May family also got involved with a carbon offset program because conserving one acre of grassland is the annual equivalent of taking 30 cars off the road.[31] The ranch sold these offsets to companies that wanted to offset their own carbon footprints which further helped the financial stability of the ranch.[32]

This is another way in which farmers, ranchers and other landowners can benefit economically while maintaining control of their land, livelihood and nest egg – all while protecting the land in perpetuity.

Summary

The divide between rural and urban America continues is real. Both sides feel misunderstood, which tends to get exacerbated during uncertain times. To change this divisive mindset and actually come together, we must focus on respect, listening and truly understanding where the "other side" is coming from. The case studies in this chapter are just a few examples of the types of win-win solutions that are out there. Unity between these two groups can be reached if we:

- Respect one another – while we may disagree with their opinions, we cannot disagree with their experiences

- Advocate for fairness – people will change when they don't feel like they are the ones having to bear all of the burden

- Visualize or walk a day in the shoes of others to empathize with their challenges

- Realize that each side's everyday lives are different, not right or wrong, just different

- Understand their anxieties and where each side is coming from

Helpful Responses	
<u>Comments</u>	<u>Response</u>
Our issues are different than yours	Yes, this is true for the specifics. But at a higher level, we all share the same basic aspirations. Let's start there!
I don't like being told what to do or being looked down upon	That is understandable, because nobody likes that! What are your biggest concerns?
(Rural) We are more concerned about preserving our livelihood than some spotted owl or gray wolf	(Urban) We are concerned about your livelihood, too. What ways do you think you will be negatively impacted by these animals? Let's work on those challenges first and see if we can come up with a win-win strategy
(Urban) Can't you see that we need immediate action to protect the environment?	(Rural) Of course we can, as we are the ones living out in nature and on the land. We just don't want to shoulder all of the burden. We want fairness
(Rural) I don't want anyone taking my guns away	(Urban) I am not advocating for anyone to take anything away. Our issues in the city are just different, can I tell you about my experience and concerns?

3: Big Business vs. Environmentalists

Big business and environmentalists are often pitted against each other. While distrust and resentment exist between the two groups, whenever the economy heads into recession businesses typically turn against environmentalists This chapter will explore why the two are traditionally in opposition and offer ways to overcome this with win-win solutions that actually improve financial performance through better environmental practices.

How can we better collaborate for a better future? How can business leaders begin to see environmentalists as insightful stakeholders who identify future opportunities and grow revenue even during uncertain times? What would it take for environmentalists to see big businesses as important partners for funding conservation/clean energy initiatives and as valuable assets to stabilize our economy, rather than as greedy and power-hungry adversaries?

Achieving this is not a pipe dream.

In fact, according to the UN Global Compact survey of 766 CEOs, 90% believe Environmental, Social and Governance (ESG) criteria need to be included into their operations and supply chain over the next five years to be successful.[33] This has been further amplified by the 180+ leaders from the Business Roundtable that proclaimed corporations exist to the benefit of all stakeholders, including customers, employees, suppliers, the community and the environment, rather than just to maximize shareholder value.

This has only been amplified by the all-hands-on-deck approach of the many corporations striving to help out and even alter their entire business model during the pandemic. There are countless examples, but here are just a few:

- Zoom, a popular online meeting platform, made their services free for K-12 schools

- General Motors shut down one of its plants to make ventilators

- Luxury goods giant LVMH repurposed its French facilities to make hand sanitizer for the government, for free.

- Verizon, Comcast and Charter all pledged not to disconnect customers who can't pay due to virus disruptions and Verizon even offered additional data for free

All of these solutions would have been laughed at by Wall Street and probably shot down by the boards of directors years ago, but these companies realize the business value in also working to sustain our society and economy. Clearly, business leaders are no longer solely interested in maximizing shareholder value and this chapter will demonstrate how implementing better environmental practices can be a win-win for the planet and company's bottom-line all at the same time.

Before we jump into those solutions though, let's first understand the points of disagreement between both groups, because if we want to have success for the long-term, we need to address these underlying concerns.

The financial perspective

The usual refrain you hear from hardcore business types is that they can't worry about environmental issues right now because they have to worry about the bottom line and just keeping their business afloat. This is because many business leaders were trained under the old Milton Friedman adage that 'the social responsibility of a corporation is to maximize shareholder value.' That means that if you are spending money on social or environmental programs, you aren't acting in the best fiduciary responsibility of an organization's shareholders.

These Milton Friedman-types want an economy with low taxes, market certainty, no new regulation and a competitive business environment. They stereotype environmentalists as obstructionists who are ill-informed as to how things truly work in an economy and how taxes and regulations hinder business growth and job creation. This narrow perspective misses the fact that most environmentalists live in the same capitalist economy as they do, with the same consumer purchasing habits that they have.

The environmentalist perspective

Environmentalists typically stereotype big business as corporate titans who are focused on making money above all else. They stigmatize businesspeople as not caring about the planet or the future they will leave to their children. For many environmentalists, big business is the source of the problem and needs to be controlled, regulated and taxed to help pay for the clean-up of the damage they've done.

It's no wonder that animosity exists if both sides have such distrust for one another. It doesn't have to be this way, though. In fact, many businesses are actually increasing sales, revenue and enhancing shareholder value through better social and environmental practices. Similarly, many environmental NGOs are benefitting from closer partnerships with business.

"We need to provide a more positive vision for the world we want to achieve instead of being a movement against things."

– Dave Phemister [34]

Misaligned incentives and compensation are to blame

How did we get to this position of constant misunderstanding and generalizing?

While there is some truth to the sentiments exhibited above, much of the reason for their existence is much simpler – misaligned compensation and evaluation criteria.

Many investors and business leaders are actually sympathetic to environmentalists' concerns about climate change, ocean plastic, deforestation and a whole handful of other issues, but are not being evaluated or rewarded based on these issues. They are being evaluated and compensated mostly by the traditional metrics of financial performance, profitability and a company's stock price. For many, it's not that they don't care about the environment, it's just that these traditional criteria are what pay the bills and lead to bonuses.

This is slowly changing though. Customers, vendors and investors are increasingly asking about environmental issues as well, which is forcing these company leaders to strive for better performance. In fact, I've had many managers tell me off the record that if ESG performance were a bigger component for how their company was being evaluated by Wall Street and investors, they would turn their company on a dime.

The myth of lower earnings

One hindrance to this common ground between these two sides is the myth that a company or investor inevitably has to sacrifice financial performance and be willing to accept lower earnings to act in a more environmentally friendly manner.

The reality is that this myth is downright false, as I'll show you below.

If you look at the performance of sustainable indices such as the Dow Jones Sustainability Index (DJSI) and S&P ESG Index versus their traditional counterparts – the Dow Jones Industrial Average (referred to as the Dow) and the S&P 500, the sustainable indices outperform the traditional ones. This has been the case for the past dozen years – through both good and bad times, before and after the 2008 recession and even during the historic performance of the market from 2017-2019, and then as recently as February 2020 before the coronavirus truly hit in the US. You can see the comparatively higher values in bold on the following page:

	S&P 500 Environmental & Socially Responsible Total Return Index[35]	S&P 500 (traditional)[36]
1 Year Annual Returns	**26.46%** ▲	24.72% ▲
3 Year Annual Returns	**14.13%** ▲	13.06% ▲
5 Year Annual Returns	**10.26%** ▲	9.94% ▲

	Dow Jones Sustainability US Index[37]	Dow Jones Industrial Average (traditional)[38]
1 Year Annual Returns	**24.90%** ▲	18.07% ▲
3 Year Annual Returns	**13.83%** ▲	13.34% ▲
5 Year Annual Returns	10.14% ▲	**10.40%** ▲

Only a month later, in March of 2020, the differences were even greater. Due to the financial collapse that resulted from the coronavirus outbreak, the regular Dow showed 1 Year Annual Returns as being down -23.21%, versus the DJSI which was only down -8.81%. Similarly, the S&P 500 was down 15.35%, and the S&P 500 ESG was down a lower amount – 11.66%. This shows that ESG investing is also more resilient during a pandemic.

Lastly, another research report that further debunks this myth was put out by AT Kearney that showed that investors are increasingly rewarding companies with ESG policies in place. It found that companies committed to these practices outperformed those that didn't by around $650 million in market capitalization during both good and uncertain times.[39]

Acting in a more environmentally responsible manner is good for business and investors.

As Anne Kelly, the Vice President of Government Affairs of BICEP/CERES states, "Caring about the environment is great, but you need to make the business case to create more constructive action with companies."[33]

Institutional investors and banks

Environmentalists also now have allies on Wall Street and in the private equity markets.

Large institutional investors such as Blackrock, Goldman Sachs, Bloomberg and State Street have put major ESG criteria into their investor analysis and Institutional Shareholder Services (ISS) has helped move the needle by sending ESG performance requests to its largest publicly traded companies.

Organizations such as the CDP (formerly known as the Carbon Disclosure Project) have found that companies that excel on social and environmental issues demonstrate a higher return on equity in terms of financial performance. In fact, from 2011-2018, the STOXX Global Climate Leaders index, based on the CDP A List, outperformed the STOXX Global 1800 of major firms by 5.4% per year.[40]

And if you think the CDP is some simple NGO questionnaire, you'd be mistaken. The market capitalization of all the companies reporting to the CDP is over $100 trillion in assets, which is greater than the gross domestic product (GDP) of the United States, China, the European Union, Japan, India and Russia *combined*.

Banks are also getting involved, as more than 100 of the world's largest banks now follow a set of guidelines called the Equator Principles. This requires organizations to proactively mitigate their own environmental and community impacts *before* getting large infrastructure loans.

The point is, there is common ground to be had. If all one cares about is maximizing shareholder value, then socially and environmentally responsible funds are one way to achieve that goal. Letitia Webster,

Chief Sustainability Officer & Partner at Mission Driven Capital Partners advises that "We need to think about big environmental problems, be it plastic or water, as simply a business/economic problem and identify the business solution."[41]

ESG is also about avoiding risk

Just as important as return on investment (ROI), investment firms are equally (if not more) focused on mitigating risk to their portfolios.

If you are able to explain to a fund manager that having stock in a coal company could lead to a decrease in their investment portfolio by 25% within the next 3 years, this will carry way more weight than a conversation about the climate impacts that the coal industry is causing. Or, if you relate to them by talking about how having an oversized portion of their portfolio in oil or airlines stocks could harm their portfolio, you'll definitely have their ear.

As Patrick Drum, Portfolio Manager and Senior Analyst at Saturna Capital is fond of saying, "When you talk about both fiduciary responsibility and embedded risks, this is the carrot-and-stick language that most Wall Street types understand."[42]

Business benefits when engaging environmentalists

Rather than seeing environmentalists as a hindrance to their business objectives, business leaders need to proactively reach out to them and see how they can be an *asset*. By listening to environmentalists, a business can be more aware of new risks, hot spots or potential regulations that may be coming down the pipe.

Look no further than how businesses leaned into solutions that were originally coming from environmentalists at the onset of the pandemic. We witnessed companies shift their entire business model overnight on issues they had rejected just weeks earlier, with mandatory work from home policies for office workers, travel bans and switching to all virtual meetings & conferences. All of these options not only helped with social distancing, but also has an environmental benefit of lowering emissions while saving money at the same time.

Environmentalists are stakeholders, so asking for their help in identifying solutions can lead to innovation, new products or a new way of delivering services. Moreover, if an Executive reaches out and says, "help show us the way," this can help turn them into allies by providing them with a forum to bring their issues/solutions to the forefront.

The dollars pencil out on a grand scale, too!

When it comes to a much broader subject like climate change, the economics are also in favor of taking action sooner rather than later. According to reports done by the Nicolas Stern Commission in the UK, the costs to abide by the Paris Climate Agreement would result in a 1-2% reduction of global GDP, but inaction or 'business as usual' could result in this costing upwards of 10% of global GDP by 2050.[43] For comparison purposes, the economic impact of the Great Recession lowered US GDP by 4.3%.

Young people are demanding action

Business and environmentalists align when it comes to engaging the upcoming generation. Both millennials and Generation Z want to work at companies that take meaningful action on environmental issues. Here are a few statistics taken of younger generations with millennials being those born between 1981-1996 and Gen Z between 1997-2012.

- 90% of Gen Z believe that companies need to take action on big social and environmental issues

- 93% of Gen Z say that companies need to walk the talk

- 88% of graduate students and young professionals factor an employer's social & environmental position into their job decision

- 95% of Gen Z will double check to see if you are meeting your commitments

- 86% of graduate students and young professionals would consider leaving a job if their employer's CSR performance no longer held up[44]

It's not just millennials and Gen Z. The Global Strategy Group's annual Business & Politics Study found that 81% of *all* Americans continue to believe that corporations should take action to address important issues facing society. [45] Look no further than the goodwill that was generated by companies who shifted their production during the coronavirus pandemic.

Agreeing on not wanting more pollution

Environmentalists who understand that most business leaders are seeking lower taxes, less regulation and a more competitive business environment can use this lens as a starting point to find win-win solutions for all – even on pollution!

For example, back in 2008, environmentalists from British Columbia wanted action on climate change while the business community was looking for payroll tax relief to stimulate hiring. Before proposing a regulatory solution, the BC government performed outreach to a diverse group of business and community stakeholders to see if they could find a win-win solution. They focused on scenarios which would provide less of what they didn't want – pollution and taxes – and more of what they desired – more jobs, cleaner air and a reduction in GHG emissions.

By focusing on their shared aspirations, businesses and environmentalists were able to start from a constructive place, rather than one of anticipated animosity. The carbon tax initiative was an easy win for most businesses which didn't have direct GHG emissions, because it lowered their payroll taxes and shifted the tax burden towards the ones actually doing the polluting. This allowed them to hire more full-time employees and created a more competitive business environment. Polluting businesses were financially incentivized to clean up their act, which resulted in everyone getting cleaner air and lowered emissions.[46] As a result, the BC carbon tax managed to meet its goals while growing GDP by 19% within the first ten years of its existence.[47]

Case studies: The environmental solution is cheaper

Mangroves in New Orleans

One of the reasons that the storm surge was so strong when Hurricane Katrina hit New Orleans, was that the mangrove swamps and barrier islands that acted as the city's natural defenses had been removed to facilitate shipping lanes in the years and decades prior.

To the average person, preserving mangrove swamps isn't a topic that comes up in everyday conversation. If you mention how it impacts real people in the context of a hurricane, the topic becomes much more interesting and relatable. For example, mangrove forests can reduce storm surges between 26-76%[48] and provide greater resiliency and protection from hurricanes at a lower cost to taxpayers, while also bringing back much needed habitat for birds and fish.

When rebuilding and protecting New Orleans after Hurricane Katrina, the Army Corps of Engineers added new levees, but it also started replanting its mangrove forests. By paying attention to those natural benefits, the levees were better reinforced while bringing back natural habitat at a lower cost than pouring more concrete.[49]

Natural stormwater treatment

Another similar example of environmental and economic benefit is the effort to clean up the Duwamish River in Seattle. This heavily industrialized area was home to cement factories, metal foundries and numerous other facilities – including Boeing's plant #2 which was used to build B-17s during World War II. It was one of the most polluted urban waterways in the United States because whenever it rained the stormwater would drain all the metals, oils and chemicals from the large impervious concrete pads straight into the river.

When local officials looked at cleaning it up, they immediately went to the traditional solution of building a wastewater treatment facility that would have cost nearly $1 billion. Both environmentalists and local business thought that there had to be a better way forward. Together, a collaboration of companies, NGOs, city government, local tribes and community members launched an initiative to utilize a massive natural restoration project to clean up the stormwater instead.[50] Natural filters and bioswales totaling almost five acres of mudflat, marsh, and riparian vegetation were planted and restored. Not only did the project stop the stormwater runoff from getting into the river, but it cost less than half of what the wastewater facility would have cost while providing a revived habitat for fish and wildlife.[51]

These are the type of win-win scenarios that make both environmental and financial sense. They allow both sides to see past their superficial differences and find common ground through practical solutions. Instead of wasting time arguing over viewpoints, these groups skipped right to finding solutions and found paths that benefitted all parties.

Environmental solutions can increase resiliency

Working from home

For example, environmentalists have long suggested business policies to include work from home (WFH) options. This reduces commuting, which reduces the wear and tear on employees sitting in traffic while lowering greenhouse gas emissions. It also can increase employee productivity and reduces office energy use and waste. However, when Coronavirus broke out across the country, WFH had another benefit – resiliency. Companies that had these policies and systems in place proved to be more resilient and had an easier time transitioning to a full-time telework schedule with less interruption to their business.

Moreover, it helped leaders who previously worried about employees slacking off when working from home to realize something I've always said – a good employee is a good employee, and a bad employee is a bad employee that'll slack off whether they are working from home or in the office.

Virtual meetings

Another example of this is the explosion in virtual meetings and conferences. For 15 years I've been working with companies on ways to reduce their GHG emissions – with business travel being one of the easiest and most cost effective ways of doing that. To a "T", I've been told by one executive team after another about the importance of face to face meetings, and that travel was too important to them. However, once the risk of spreading the virus during the pandemic became known, most businesses switched all of their meetings and conferences to virtual ones almost immediately.

These two examples may at first seem only like environmental solutions, but they reduce both costs and risks to the business, as well as increase the productivity of their workforce by focusing their time on work instead of commuting and travel.

Summary

A myth has been perpetuated over the last four decades that taking positive steps to protect the environment will hurt the economy, lead to job losses and negatively impact businesses. This chapter debunked that mindset and provided numerous win-win strategies that protect the planet while leading to higher business profits.

The reality is that while action on environmental issues like climate change and ocean plastics are stalled in Congress, big business is paying attention and taking action all around us. If business types and environmentalists can shed their traditional "us vs. them" mentality, there is an opportunity for both sides to collectively meet their goals.

To accomplish this, we must:

- Showcase examples of where business benefitted by working with environmentalists to solve their challenges, like how investment indices like the DJSI and S&P ESG Index outperform their traditional counterparts

- Empathize with the importance of putting an issue into the other person's language by focusing on what they care about, as opposed to what compels you

- Remind yourself that ESG performance is now how many companies are being evaluated in addition to financial metrics

- Understand that misaligned incentives, evaluation criteria and compensation packages are partly responsible when business does not take environmental action

- Realize that environmentalists are also consumers who have homes, cars and jobs and that most businesspeople have had a positive experience with nature to reminisce about

- See that environmental solutions often have other benefits, like being saving money and increasing resiliency

- Note that business is way more influenced and driven by market and investor behavior than moral/ environmental arguments

The tables on the following pages are different from other chapters' "Helpful Responses" in that they highlight what people in different departments tend to care about most, and then offer potential environmental responses. Businesses can use this as a tool to find ways through roadblocks and environmentalists can use this to learn how to put their issues into the language of business.

Helpful Responses
Businesses have multiple departments, each with their own priorities, so this table is broken down by functional area to provide more context. Departments are in **bold**.

Comments	Responses
Investor Relations:	_They care about:_ Maintaining their stock price and reducing volatility
We need to maximize shareholder value	The Dow Jones Sustainability Index and the S&P 500 ESG Index actually outperformed the Dow and S&P 500 over the past 11 years
Shareholders are not demanding that we act sustainability, especially during times of economic & public health uncertainty	There are now Securities & Exchange Commission (SEC) guidelines that require disclosure on climate change
	Intangible benefits like increased brand value, competitive advantage and goodwill are improving shareholder value and are something that stakeholders care about as well

Finance/ Accounting/CFO:	*They care about: The bottom-line financials of the company*
This is going to cost more, and I need to focus on the bottom-line	The business case shows both short-term and long-term ROIs. There are numerous low-hanging fruit opportunities in the short term that save $$, like energy efficiency
We need to see a quick payback	Why? What other projects are held to such a quick payback period? What payback was required for diversity or sexual harassment education?

Legal:	*They care about: Reducing and eliminating risk. They think through the lens of avoiding risk*
We don't want to open ourselves up to extra scrutiny or exposure	By paying attention to potential social and environmental risks, you might actually be reducing your liability over the long term. Also, legal experts suggest that disclosing risk lowers liability by creating a more defensible position: "We told you." Think about how you viewed risk before vs. after COVID-19
If people aren't asking, let's not volunteer information	Don't be afraid to show the good work you've done. If you are worried about being attacked, engage an NGO or friendly stakeholder to provide 'air cover' for you. You don't have to have solved every risk, but it is important to demonstrate that you are taking issues seriously and have a strategy

Operations/ Facilities:	*They care about:* The operational performance of the buildings they manage. They lack capital resources to implement all the water, waste and efficiency solutions they want to deploy
We have no budget	We should start with the no-cost and low-cost initiatives first. We can use the earnings from those small changes to help pay for some of the bigger, costlier solutions
I don't have time to deal with this and don't want to be told how to do my job	Of course, you know your job better than anyone. I just think these case studies could make your life easier, since the sustainability initiatives saved money and increased efficiency

Supply Chain:	*They care about:* Making sure the goods and services get to their destination as efficiently, safely and inexpensively as possible
We're not a big enough fish to influence change	If not, then partner with others in your industry. For example, many outdoor retailers use the same suppliers and factories in China; they sometimes band together to create a critical mass on an issue they'd like changed
	You could invite suppliers to a conference where you explain your sustainability goals/vision. Ask them for ways that they can help you achieve your goals

Human Resources:	*They care about:* Attracting great employees and retaining their best employees
Show me how this will help with retention and recruitment	Millennial/Gen Z employees expect action on the environment. Other companies are using this to attract next generation talent
This won't be worth the cost	Losing a good employee can cost between 70% and 200% of current pay, and close to 80% of millennials may leave a company if it abandons its environmental efforts
We can't afford sustainability benefits	Most benefits are sustainability related already, they are just called "Health and Wellness." Offer them a suite of 4-5 to choose from (i.e. gym membership, bus pass, free yoga, etc.). Working from home, which became essential during COVID-19, counts as one of these benefits!

Sales & Marketing:	_They care about:_ Selling more of their goods and services, and are looking for additional entry-points to sway customers
There is no market, or the market is unproven	There is ample market data, and LOHAS (lifestyle of health and sustainability) statistics show millennial/Gen Z consumer preferences are towards products that share their values. Newer markets provide opportunities for first-mover advantage and are a way to build out top-line revenue growth
Current customers are not asking for sustainability	What is the last time you asked your customers about these issues? Consumer sentiment is reacting more and more favorably towards taking action on social and environmental issues. More likely than not, their opinions have changed in recent years

4: Climate Skeptics vs. Climate Advocates

Is climate change happening? Are humans to blame? Is it real, a hoax, or the greatest crisis of our generation?

The way these disagreements play out in Congress, across social media and on cable news networks, prevents us from making progress and moving forward. This chapter comes from a neutral angle and explains why that is, shows how we can overcome these sentiments and provides common ground examples that are win-wins between these divergent viewpoints.

Terms defined

Just so we are all starting on the same page, here are clarifications of the terms we will be using throughout this chapter:

CLIMATE	Long-term weather patterns, temperature and humidity in a specific place – over periods of time usually averaging 30 years or more
WEATHER	Day-to-day changes in temperature and precipitation that are short-term – over hours, days and weeks
CLIMATE SKEPTICS	People who don't believe that the science behind man-made climate change is proven and believe that the Earth has been naturally warming and cooling for millions of years
CLIMATE ADVOCATES	People who believe that climate change is occurring, that it is being made worse by human activity and it is an existential threat to people and the planet

This is a controversial issue, as people vary from thinking that this is a non-issue or not our most immediate concern right now, while others see it as *the* existential threat to our species.

Therefore, I ask you to please read this with an open mind and a kind heart. It will be uncomfortable at times to read arguments that you disagree with, but remember that it is part of the process of what we're trying to do with this book. We need to learn to hear from the "other side" to move things forward for the betterment of our families – no matter which side your opinions fall on.

The main arguments

Climate skeptics dispute the existence of global warming. They question whether extreme weather events are tied to climate change and tend to believe that it is a naturally occurring phenomena rather than caused by human behavior. Moreover, many of them feel like they are the ones whose lives will be most negatively impacted by climate action, and they often feel disrespected by advocates for their views.

An argument that skeptics use is that changes in the climate have always happened, and it may even have possible benefits as well. For example, warmer winters mean longer agricultural seasons and potentially more revenue for farmers, as well as providing opportunities to plant crops at more northern latitudes.

Climate advocates, on the other hand, believe that climate change is *the* existential threat to mankind and that it is already manifesting in extreme weather events, as well as disproportionally affecting disadvantaged populations. They point to the increase in hurricane frequency and intensity of forest fires in Australia, California and the Amazon rainforest as evidence. Climate advocates believe the science and, in their minds, the evidence proves that climate change is clearly man-made. Their concern goes so deep that sometimes they project that climate skeptics don't care about the mutual well-being of their children and the future we leave for them.

The type of media coverage that climate change receives also differs between the more extreme left or right-leaning media channels – as both try to appeal to their respective audiences. Because of this imbalance, a polarized distrust has developed on the accuracy of the information that is being presented.

This leads to both sides repeating their arguments over and over and with these mental barriers in place, neither side is getting through to the other. Why are we having such a hard time moving forward? Are there solutions in which it doesn't even matter if they agree?

It's not about the science

I've come to realize that on this issue, people largely form their beliefs based on emotion, personal experience and values. This is where we need to start our conversations – not by arguing over the facts or science, because there are deeper underlying emotions at play that need to be addressed first, which I explore below.

Underlying anxieties

Climate change causes anxiety, fear and frustration on both sides.

Skeptics, who are often already distrustful of government and the media, believe that action on climate will negatively impact their way of life, financials or communities – whether it's through the vehicle they drive, the food they eat or energy they use. There are some skeptics who argue that the Earth is actually headed towards the next ice age. Many skeptics believe that there are more pressing social or economic issues that should be addressed before worrying about the possibility of sea-level rise or a 2 degree Celsius increase in temperature.

Advocates, on the other hand, tend to believe that if they just keep showing scientific evidence and facts, that skeptics will eventually "get it." They feel anxious and worried about the environment, species eradication and what their kid's lives will be like in the future if drastic action isn't taken immediately. Constantly hearing about potential devastation and negative impacts can even lead to feeling overwhelmed – a phenomenon known as "climate fatigue." While some take to the streets in a call for action, others become numb and shut down because they are paralyzed by how massive the problem is.

A business owner may fall in either camp, but their concerns likely lie in the middle somewhere, with concerns centered around what the costs of action may mean to the bottom line of their business. They want to know:

- Can I afford this?

- Will I have to lay off employees to comply with this?

- Will I have to change how I do things?

- Will what I do even matter if the government doesn't take decisive action?

- If there is this much uncertainty, how do I know if this is a smart business decision?

It starts with listening

Each side's anxiety is real and needs to be given credence. While we may disagree with someone's opinion, we cannot disagree with their personal experiences. As I expressed previously, it's important to empathize and genuinely try to understand the concerns of the "other side" rather than trying to convince them why you are right.

This is what is missed by advocates and skeptics alike. Both staunchly believe that the other side is wrong and should listen *to them*.

This may seem overly simplistic, but it is the truth. The key to getting past this is through *authentic listening*. Before trying to pound your position with facts, figures or snowballs, ask them why they believe what they do.

Being an authentic listener will help you further the conversation beyond the traditional talking points. By listening to what is behind their thoughts you can get to the core of their concerns and look for areas of common ground. Without doing this, you have no idea how negatively your "great solution" may affect them personally.

Climate is not just a left vs. right issue; it's a generational one

When did clean air, clean water and a thriving natural environment become a partisan issue? In 1988, the Republican President George Herbert Walker Bush ran as our "Environmental President." You'd probably forgotten or perhaps never realized that.

More recently though, Republicans and Democrats have forged drastically divergent opinions around the issue of climate change in their party platforms. The media tends to stereotype it as a "Democrats care and Republicans don't" narrative, but the reality is actually more nuanced, as the core of the discussion is now rooted in generational differences.[52]

Millennials and Gen Z not only grew up with smart-phones and ubiquitous access to Wi-Fi, they also grew up with recycling, composting and taking care of the environment. These things are normal for them and they are the ones that would be most affected by climate change. Studies show that 20% of Americans age 23-38 say that climate change is the most important issue facing the country, which is double that of those 39-54 years old at 9%.[53]

More interestingly, a recent poll by Ipsos & Newsy showcases this generational gap with percentages of people who agreed with the following statement:

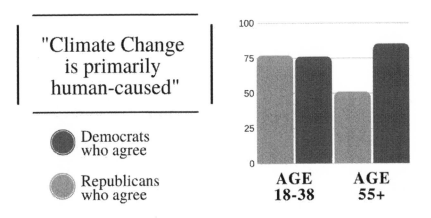

As you can see, younger Republicans and Democrats share the exact same sentiment about climate change. While there is a huge generational difference in opinion, the percentage of young Republicans (77%) who believe that climate change is caused by humans was not only equal to, but even slightly above the Democrats (76%) for millennials/Gen Z.[54]

This is what Benji Backer addresses in his work, as one of the leading voices on this issue for young conservatives. The only Republican witness at the Congressional climate change hearing in 2019, Backer sat at the table with Greta Thunberg, spoke on climate change and won Forbes' 30 under 30: Energy Award soon after.

Backer believes that a market-based approach will best address climate change – and he is not the only conservative to think this. He remarks, "There are a lot of people out there who would probably vote Republican if they knew there was a conservative agenda on climate change," and warns, "Right now they're going to the Democratic Party, because that's the only party that's talking about the environment."[55]

Where common ground exists

Extreme weather events

People disagree about climate change, but one area where common ground can be found is through their personal experience of dealing with an extreme weather event. In fact, almost every individual in the US has been affected by one of these in the last five years – whether it be a forest fire, flood, hurricane, bomb cyclone, drought, blizzard or polar vortex. It is much easier to relate with someone about these types of extreme events than it is to talk about sea-level rise or the threat to the polar ice caps.

Everyone has their own story to tell about how an event impacted their lives, their business or their daily routine. From heat waves in the Southeast to droughts across the West (where the term "fire season" has now become a normalized term), people have new expectations for weather disruption. For example, Houston experienced three once-every-thousand-year floods in just a five-year span of time, which obviously isn't supposed to happen – hence the name.

The following graphic shows the extreme weather events from 2019 that caused over a billion dollars in damage:[56] If this graphic was expanded to include damages from events that just caused millions or even tens of millions of dollars, almost every state would have an image on it, and 2019 was a relatively tame year.

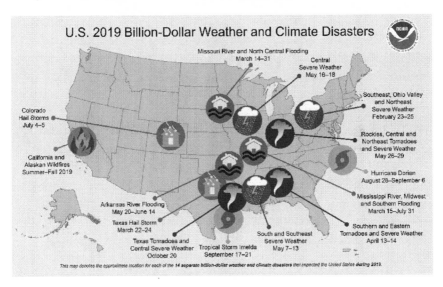

There will be disagreement as to how the climate has changed, why it's occurring and whether it is good or bad, but there is consensus that things are different. Without even approaching a conversation about the reasons why it has changed, people will often open up about how they were individually affected by one of these events. There may have been disruptions to their children or family, lost wages, repairs that needed to be made to their house or destruction of infrastructure in their community from forest fires, floods, hurricanes and blizzards.

People can relate to shared experiences just like how everyone can relate to each other around the Coronavirus and economic fallout. By first focusing on shared experiences, you can work towards win-

win solutions to avoid or limit impacts from extreme weather events in the future.

Use hope instead of fear

Some advocates think that showing a sad image of a starving polar bear will inspire action, whereas skeptics tend to believe that talking about how action on climate will lead to job losses and economic stagnation advances their side of the argument.

The reality is that fearful or negative messaging isn't successful on either side. These images have the exact opposite effect; instead of getting someone to engage, in fact, it either paralyzes them or prompts an eye roll. Both sides need to promote a message of hope instead.

We need to flip the switch and demonstrate opportunity and possibility. We need to show solutions that can improve the quality of life for the person you are talking to – things that benefit their business, family and/or community. One can deny causation, but cleaner air, water and a more prosperous life is hard to argue against. The following pages provide win-win solutions that bring that mindset into action, no matter which side you are on.

But what if it's all one big hoax?

I was once asked this question in Oregon by a businessman at a conference. I responded to this individual, "Why wouldn't you want to do things that could save your business money, energy, water and waste? What if your actions on climate change, whether it's real or not, helped you keep your best employees and attract the most innovative young minds? What if you were able to reduce risk and enhance your brand value all at the same time?"

These are financially beneficial results that help both business and the environment, whether you believe in climate change or not.

This doesn't even include the idea of how renewable energy could lead us towards energy independence and further decouple us from the conflicts in the Middle East, or other benefits such as species protection, rainforest preservation, fewer extreme weather events and lower cases of asthma & eczema in humans. So, when someone asks the "what if" from a negative perspective, be sure to focus on the positive benefits that proactive action could provide.

Win-win solutions

You can't disagree with the bottom line

Building off the case studies offered in the Big Business vs. Environmentalists chapter, one way to cut through the ideology of both sides around climate change is simply to focus on the financial bottom line. To lower the ideological temperature, don't talk science, morals or ideology. Talk money.

For example, a friend of mine at a large agricultural company was a climate advocate while his CEO was a climate skeptic. This obviously led to great disagreement until they set their ideologies aside and focused on bottom line financial impacts to their business.

Instead of talking about the science, they discussed what they thought were the biggest long-term threats to their company. It was clear in a matter of minutes that to this agricultural company, there was nothing more important than access to water and healthy soil. So, instead of arguing over the reality of climate change, they talked about the financial risks that increased droughts and water scarcity could have on their future harvests.

This led them to embrace innovative irrigation techniques that used smart phone sensors to give plants the right amount of water at exactly the time they needed it. Instead of watering first thing in the morning or in the early evening to avoid evaporation, they would instead provide water to each plant exactly when it needed it most. This strategy saved energy, water and (most importantly to their CEO) money, while also improving their harvests and long-term water risk. This was a win-win solution that was achieved even though they held opposite ideologies on climate change.

One person's trash is another's treasure

The following examples exist in just one city, to show the multitude of possibilities all around us.

Baseball

Unless it snows on opening day or during the World Series, you don't tend to think of Major League Baseball when you think about climate change. However, the Seattle Mariners found an innovative way to reduce GHG emissions, improve the grass on their field and save money at the same time. The Mariners play in T-Mobile Park, which has a retractable roof to protect from rain but is not a fully enclosed stadium. This means that in the winter, the temperature in the stadium and grass-growing conditions are less than ideal.

The Mariners partnered with Seattle Public Utilities to route its wastewater line (which stays at about 50 degrees Fahrenheit) under the field to help heat the stadium and keep the soil warm. This reduced energy use and GHG emissions while improving the playing surface by helping the grass grow. Unfortunately, this hasn't done anything yet to improve the team's crappy performance on the field!

Beer

Fremont Brewing is a fun win-win example on climate. Brewing beer uses a lot of heat and the traditional way of getting rid of this excess heat was to just release it into the open air. However, this small brew pub was located next to a Bikram yoga studio that needed large amounts of heat for its classes and was also looking for a way to lower its natural gas bill. The two companies worked together to build a system that captured the brewing company's waste heat and pumped it directly into the yoga studio. As a result, the yoga studio saved money and the brewery was paid for a previously unused asset. Both companies improved financially while using less energy and lowering emissions.

Starbucks

Starbucks was looking for ways to lower both its waste footprint and waste disposal costs. Coffee grounds are heavy and since waste is usually billed by weight, anything that the company could do to reduce the amount of coffee grounds ending up in its waste stream would save the company money.

Starbucks found a way to vacuum seal its used coffee grounds at its stores, and because this is a very effective fertilizer for gardeners, customers actually show up and take it away for free. This saves the company money, lowers emissions by putting the coffee grounds back into productive use as a natural fertilizer and reduces the company's waste footprint at the same time. Starbucks has found a way to entice their customers to literally come to their stores and help haul away their trash!

Differentiating your brand through leadership

The two-time MLS Cup Champions Seattle Sounders FC professional soccer team has taken action on climate change as a way to connect with its fans, demonstrate brand leadership and even open up potential new community partnerships. How did they do this?

My firm, Sustainable Business Consulting, helped the Sounders 1) calculate its GHG inventory, 2) identify ways to reduce their GHG impacts where they could, and 3) coordinate carbon offsets for the club to purchase for the remainder of its footprint. As you can imagine, a pro team can't stop traveling to its opponents to keep its GHG emissions down, so offsets became a necessary part of the solution.

By doing this, the Sounders became the first US pro team to become carbon neutral, receiving significant publicity because of the commitment. They even went a step further. They didn't just purchase the offsets, they actually put the trees into the ground themselves by partnering with a local conservation group, Forterra. Sounders FC invited their fans, players, coaches, sponsors, and community partners to join them in planting trees that would help clean up the air and water that all of these stakeholders use. This was a win for the environment and a win for the Sounders.

These are just a few examples, and many more win-win solutions exist where taking action on climate change was not only better for the planet, but also for the business bottom line. I encourage you to keep an eye out for money-saving opportunities like these in your own life, work and community.

Summary

Climate change has become a hyper-politicized issue, with each side firmly entrenched in their own views. By seeking to truly understand what is at the core of each side's beliefs, we can begin to find common ground and take action in ways that benefit everyone involved. To move forward, each side needs to stop finger-pointing and start listening for opportunities to bridge this divide. To do this:

- Identify win-win, market-based solutions that address the economic anxieties of skeptics while delivering greenhouse gas reductions for advocates

- Don't talk about climate, but do talk about extreme weather events and ask the person you are talking to how they may have been personally impacted

- Realize that presenting more scientific data and facts will not change someone's mind

- Pay attention to the generational gap as much as the political one, as millennials and Gen Z are non-partisan on climate

- Talk solutions and emphasize hope instead of fear

- Understand that this topic is about more than just temperature increases – it also has consequences that are social, political, economic and cultural

- Engage all stakeholders, because different communities have different priorities

Helpful Responses	
<u>Comments</u>	<u>Response</u>
The science (does or does not prove)	Regardless, did you know that there are win-win solutions that address your specific needs and anxieties, as well as mine? Let's focus on those!
(Advocate) Humans are to blame for climate change	(Skeptic) Climate change is caused by the natural warming and cooling of the Earth and this has been happening for millions of years. But I know some ways we can both get what we want...
(Skeptic) You are more concerned about saving polar bears and glaciers than people	(Advocate) It's not just about the animals – humans are also experiencing impacts. These extreme weather events have huge negative consequences on people like us and across the globe, though they may be subtle and happening slowly. For example, (insert idea here)

5. Military vs. Sustainability

The military is one of the most revered institutions in the United States and few things are perceived to be more patriotic than supporting the troops. In addition to being called upon for combat and humanitarian missions overseas, they were the first ones called upon when we needed extra hospital facilities and beds during the Coronavirus pandemic. What few know though, is that the United States Military has been on the forefront of adopting environmental solutions into its strategy for years.

When you bring up this topic though, people often question the notion and a customary refrain you hear is, "We shouldn't be putting the safety of our brave young servicemen and women at risk, just to be green!"

This isn't what this chapter is about, because nobody actually advocates for that. The reality is that the US military has been on the forefront of several environmental initiatives – embracing renewables, leading on hybrid technologies and adopting energy & water saving measures – not because it is the right thing to do, but because it saves money and frees up other assets to improve combat readiness and operational resiliency.

All the way back in 2004 the Pentagon determined climate change to be "*the* greatest threat to US national security over the next 50 years." Therefore, to the military, this isn't some 'green' issue – climate change and its environmental, social and economic impacts are a threat to global stability.[57]

When asked about what environmental resilience means to the military, retired Army Colonel and former Chief of US Army Operational Energy Office Paul Roege put it best. He says these efforts improve the military's ability to thrive under changing situations and recover from deliberate attacks, accidents or naturally occurring threats.[58]

In fact, if you go back and look at propaganda materials created during World War II, the notion of patriotism was strongly related to environmental conservation. Similar to the way Americans bonded together through the shared sacrifices they made to get through the Pandemic most recently, back in the 1940s the government asked all Americans to pitch in and donate rubber from their cars for reuse in the war effort, to plant victory gardens to free up food for the troops and even created posters like the one below.[59]

As you can see, environmental conservation and patriotism were one and the same during World War II. Tap into this history when trying to find common ground going forward.

Solar panels save lives

The Army and Marines have both turned to portable solar power to reduce the weight and amount of batteries carried by soldiers and to lower the number of casualties related to fuel transports.

They did this because at the beginning of the Afghanistan War, a large number of casualties were tied directly to the transportation of diesel fuel. In addition to powering vehicles, almost 40% of this fuel was being converted into electricity to power batteries for radios, communication devise, GPS systems, laptops and electronic warfare tools in the field.[60]

In 2009, the Marines started deploying portable solar arrays to reduce the amount of batteries soldiers were carrying in the field by as much as 25 lbs.[61] As you can imagine, this made a huge difference in terms of agility and speed when climbing up 13,000 foot peaks or in a fire fight with the Taliban. Moreover, lighter packs reduced back injuries and because the solar panels generated sufficient energy during the day, this enabled the command posts to cut diesel consumption from their generators from 20 gallons/day to 2.5 gallons/day.[62]

At the start of the war, nearly 1-in-3 casualties were associated with fuel convoys. After solar was embraced, lower diesel demands lessened the number of casualties associated with fuel and the number dropped to 1-in-9.[63] In addition, soldiers could be redeployed from transporting and escorting fuel convoys to other critical areas.

This adoption of portable solar units had an additional social benefit in that it sometimes generated *excess* power, which could be provided to local villagers to charge mobile phones & devices and helped build camaraderie between the soldiers and the local community.

The Navy leads the way

The Navy has been on the forefront of technological environmental initiatives such as biofuels and hybrid-electric propulsion systems. These efforts are designed to reduce costs, fossil fuel use and GHG emissions while simultaneously helping the Navy to deploy for longer periods of time before refueling.

One energy efficiency innovation rolled out by the Navy has been the marine hybrid electric propulsion system which is used to supplement traditional diesel engines. Not only do these burn cleaner and use less fuel, but they also provide enhanced mission capabilities.

For example, the hybrid electric propulsion system allows ships to stay out on mission an average of an extra 2.5 days before refueling. Moreover, these systems can run on electric power entirely when running below 13 knots. This lowers their sonar footprint, which is an advantage in anti-submarine warfare, while also lowering GHG emissions between 10-25% at the same time.[64]

The "Great Green Fleet"

The Navy's Great Green Fleet, a play on President Teddy Roosevelt's "Great White Fleet" which sailed around the world in the early 1900s to project American power, was designed to demonstrate that the US Navy could field the most energy efficient and modern fleet across the globe.

Piloted by the US Nimitz Carrier Strike Group during operation RIMPAC (Rim of the Pacific) in 2012, the Great Green Fleet was fully deployed in 2016. While the aircraft carrier Nimitz is nuclear powered, everything else in its strike group including aircraft ran on a 50/50 mix of traditional oil and biofuels, thus realizing the goal of a more affordable, lower emitting fleet without sacrificing any war fighting or readiness capabilities.[65]

Renewables are part of the strategy

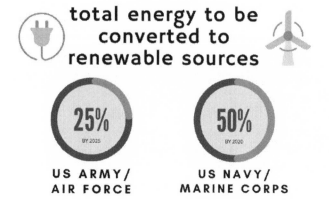

total energy to be converted to renewable sources

25%
BY 2025

US ARMY /
AIR FORCE

50%
BY 2020

US NAVY /
MARINE CORPS

These four branches of the Armed Forces in the previous graphic all set renewable energy targets to reduce their reliance on fossil fuels over the next few years, especially imported foreign oil.[66] The military's overall oil consumption fell by 20% over an eight year period, even while fighting two wars and being involved in other smaller conflicts around the globe.[67]

These savings freed up money that otherwise would have been spent on fuel and could now be reinvested into combat readiness, up-armoring Humvee's, new body armor, increased wages for our troops and many other operating priorities.

These targets are essential as the amount of fuel that is needed to support a single soldier has increased dramatically over the past few conflicts, as seen below.[68]

GALLONS TO SUPPORT ONE SOLIDER

1   20

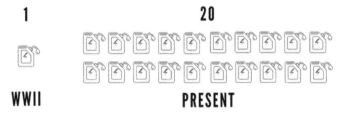

WWII   PRESENT

Summary

How the military embraces environmentalism is a great example of what kind of common ground exists between two groups that are traditionally viewed to be on the opposite ends of the spectrum. The military doesn't have time for politics and everyone is fighting on the same team – for our country. They have used environmental solutions in ways that help:

- Identify cost savings

- Use less fuel

- Reduce casualties

- Improve combat readiness

- Improve resiliency

- Protect the environment

Helpful Responses	
<u>Comments</u>	<u>Response</u>
The military shouldn't be worried about "going green," it has bigger things to worry about	Paying attention to energy and resource management frees up money for other things including combat readiness & new equipment
The Army has a job to do and it needs fuel to do it	Saving fuel saves lives. A disproportionate number of soldiers have been injured or killed escorting fuel convoys
Solar power doesn't belong on the battlefield	Solar allows troops to lighten their packs, which makes them more agile in a fire fight and provides power to their communication devices while in the field
The Navy is unrelated to environmental efforts	Hybrid electric motors enable ships to deploy up to 2.5 days longer. The electric motors also help evade sonar detection when they run under 13 knots

6. Fossil Fuels vs. Renewable Energy

"Fossil Fuels"   *"Renewable Energy"*

What is the first thing you think of when you hear these two words? What emotion is invoked?

I ask because there is tremendous apprehension on both sides of the energy equation. These fears are exacerbated by media riling up people from both sides about the effect to their jobs, their pocketbooks, the environment and their general way of life. Though this topic has taken a major backseat during the recent crisis, it is still a point of great contention and disagreement among Americans. This is yet another area that is filled with innovated win-win solutions that can help us all come together, especially for these economically distressed communities related to the coal industry.

When we move past traditional talking points and address the deeper concerns of each side, we uncover practical solutions that meet the needs of both sides of the energy equation.

Where the tension lies

The words "renewable" or "fossil fuel" are triggers. This is because both sides view the other as a direct threat to their way of life and economic situations. Tensions have grown in recent years between advocates for traditional, fossil fuel-based energy (coal, oil, natural gas) and advocates for renewable energy (solar, wind, bioenergy, etc.) as this has been exasperated as a hyper-partisan issue.

Fossil fuel advocates tend to be people who either rely on fossil fuels for their job/lifestyle or see no problem with continuing to use them. They feel threatened that a transition to clean energy may lead to higher prices, a loss of blue-collar jobs and demand changes to their current purchasing habits and way of life. Similar to climate skeptics, they are anxious about what they will be forced to give up.

Renewable energy advocates are people who encourage transitioning our society towards more renewable or "clean" energy options. They are worried about the future of the planet and believe that clean energy solutions are needed in the 21st century. They believe that our long-term security and well-being is threatened by the continued burning of fossil fuels and that jobs in clean energy over the next decade could be as big as the IT boom of the last two decades.

	Fossil Fuel Concerns	Renewable Concerns
Threats	▪ Will make it financially harder for the average American ▪ Danger to way of life	▪ Danger to the environment ▪ Urgent need to address climate change
Energy Accessibility	▪ The wind doesn't always blow, the sun doesn't always shine ▪ Range anxiety, Electric vehicle (EV) charging stations aren't every-where like gas stations	▪ Planet has limited resources ▪ Conflicts in the Middle East affect supply, cost and potentially our security
Jobs	▪ Will result in less coal/gas jobs for blue collar workers	▪ Has the potential to lead to a job revolution ▪ Are already the fastest growing jobs in the US
Fairness	▪ Worried about increased regulation ▪ Don't want special treatment for green/clean energy	▪ Want certainty that tax incentives for solar, wind, EVs will remain in place ▪ Want same subsidies as fossil fuels
Price	▪ Worried that 'clean' costs more ▪ Not everyone can afford an EV	▪ Solar and wind are now cost competitive with natural gas and cheaper than coal ▪ Need more EV infrastructure

In order to make progress though, we must explore what is at the core of each argument, address concerns about their jobs, the economy, the environment and work towards win-win solutions.

Engaging with the "other side"

Both sides have to stop demonizing the "other side" and instead engage and empathize with them. Fossil fuel advocates can be quick to assume that environmentalists are maliciously going after their family and income. Rather than based on cruel intent, renewable advocates' vision for a clean energy transition is about reducing GHG emissions while creating reliable jobs. At the same time, renewable advocates must stop saying that fossil fuel supporters are single-handedly destroying the planet. Name calling is counter-productive for both sides.

We need to flip the script. Instead of demonizing people, we need to respect, understand and honor them. For example, in the hard-hit coal regions of West Virginia, Southern Ohio, Pennsylvania and Kentucky, we need to honor the coal workers and communities who have long made sacrifices for our ability to access cheap energy. The economic hardships and job losses that their communities face are real and we all need to work towards finding solutions that make their lives better.

Assuming good intent in people completely changes how you engage with the "other side." Look in a mirror and reflect on what kinds of assumptions you have been operating on.

Realizing shared priorities

If you asked the average person on the street about their 'energy preferences,' especially during these challenging times, you likely wouldn't elicit much of a response. However, if you were to ask that same person if they want to be able to turn on their lights, heat their home, drive their car and charge their phone when they want to, they undoubtedly will say, "Yes!"

Everyone tends to agree on these basic premises, "the ends," but once again, it is "the means" that trips us up and divides us into camps, so much so that we default to despising the "other side" for getting in our way instead of getting the right things done.

Outside of the workers, investors or employees of energy companies, many people don't pay much attention to where their power or fuel comes from. They just don't want to be inconvenienced. However, if all things are equal in terms of price, performance and convenience, the average person would likely prefer the non-polluting option.

Therefore, let's return to what we can all agree that we want:

- Electricity, heat and fuel when we need it

- Reliability, accessibility and certainty of power

- Affordable prices (cheaper is better)

Many would agree that renewables are fine, but only if these other three conditions are met first.

What is driving division

"The environmental movement is killing the coal industry," is a common refrain and one of the biggest fallacies that exists in the US's cultural and media mindset. As environmentalism became increasingly politically polarized, a popular refrain from fossil fuel advocates is that coal's demise is due to environmental regulation. The truth is that the biggest factor in coal's decline has been utilities converting their power plants from coal to natural gas, simply because it is cheaper.

In fact, since 2016 coal has been more expensive than natural gas to generate and is now competitive with wind and solar.[69] Economics, in addition to technological advancements like mountain-top removal (which requires fewer workers), are more to blame for the decline of coal than environmental regulation or renewable energy advocates.[70]

We also must not lose sight of the fact that for all the attention that the loss of coal jobs gets, the truth is that there are now more people working in each of the wind and solar industries than the coal industry.[71] Hell, there are more people working at Arby's than in the coal industry, and we aren't changing public policy for Arby's!

This collapse of the coal industry mirrors what happened with the timber industry in the 1980's and 90's, where loggers felt like their livelihoods and communities were threatened by environmentalists who were trying to save the spotted owl.[72]

What was really eliminating their timber jobs, however, was new timber-harvesting technology such as the Timber Pro or the John Deer Bundler, which can cut, strip and load whole hillsides of trees onto trucks – the equivalent workload of 30 loggers – in about half the time and at about $1/4^{th}$ the cost.[73] In times of uncertainty and change, it's important to realize what the true causes are.

Win-win examples

Drawing a parallel from history

By 1993, the Soviet Union had collapsed and the Clinton Administration had decided to cut $50 billion from the defense budget. There was great concern that this would lead to massive layoffs for defense contractors. To preserve jobs and ease a technological transition, the administration decided to heavily invest in job retraining programs for these extremely talented engineers.

Nowhere was this more pronounced than with the Satellite division of aerospace defense contractor Hughes Electronics. They embraced these retraining dollars and pivoted away from defense, utilizing its satellite expertise to create DIRECTV, which opened up an entirely new business and revenue stream to the organization. It was a win-win.

More recently, Ventec Life Systems reached out to former aerospace and defense workers at Boeing when it needed experienced technicians, engineers and electricians to produce ventilators during the Coronavirus pandemic. These are parallels that can be drawn for today's fossil fuel workers as renewables are embraced.

From coal to clean energy

The workforce retraining system that was developed for defense contractors in the 1990s needs to be used today for coal miners, which lost over 30% of its workforce since 2010.[74] The miners, engineers, geologists who have been on the front lines in the coal industry could be retrained to fill new jobs in the clean energy and carbon sequestration fields for example.

For the coal industry, there are programs such as the Coalfield Development Corporation, which is a non-profit that was developed in West Virginia to support all coal jobs in Appalachia. It puts coal employees back to work on solar installation, energy efficiency projects or similar programs through the Interstate Renewable Energy Council. Jobs such as wind turbine technicians earn above the average wage for all US workers at over $54,000 annually and only require a high school diploma.[75]

While the media likes to paint the image of blue-collar jobs as only those in traditional fields such as in the fossil fuel industry, the majority of renewable energy jobs are also blue-collar. These are the types of jobs that can prop up fossil fuel communities during an economic and energy transition.

Summary

Fossil fuel defenders and renewable energy advocates are in conflict because both sides see the other as a threat to their way of life. By understanding the true concerns of both sides and addressing them with respect, Americans can find common ground between fossil fuel and renewable energy advocates to move things forward.

It is essential to identify nonpartisan solutions that deliver renewable energy jobs, while taking care of those that will be most affected by any type of transition away from fossil fuels. It can and must be done if we are to meet in the middle.

The reality is that for the average Jane or Joe, their priority is that the energy they need to charge their phones or drive a car is:

1. Reliable

2. Affordable

3. Available the moment they need it

Common ground can be found between these two sides if these three basics needs are met first and to move the conversation forward, we must:

- Realize people are resistant to change. If something works for them right now, they don't want to risk disruption to their day-to-day

- Respect and honor the hard-working communities of fossil fuel workers and address their needs and concerns

- Showcase that renewables are now cost competitive with fossil fuels

- Understand that the lower cost of natural gas and technology innovation have been the real reason coal jobs are disappearing

- Recognize that there are actually more jobs related to both solar and wind power than coal, although the compensation is different

Helpful Responses	
Comments	Response
(Fossil fuel) Renewables cost more	(Renewables) That definitely used to be the case, but recently solar and wind are actually cheaper than coal and oil, and cost competitive with natural gas
(Fossil fuel) Renewables need to stand on their own and not be subsidized by the government or taxpayers	(Renewables) Both energy sources receive subsidies. In fact, renewables receive less than 10% of what fossil fuels receive. In fact, it annually costs every US taxpayer $21 in renewable energy subsidies, and $2,008 for fossil fuels. [76]
(Fossil fuel) Environmentalists are killing coal jobs and peoples' livelihoods	(Renewables) I agree that coal is becoming an unstable industry, but the lower price of natural gas is what is really killing it – utilities are shifting from coal power to natural gas due to cost. We need to find transition opportunities for fossil fuel coal workers
(Renewables) Solar and wind are some of the fastest growing jobs in the country	(Fossil fuel) This may be true, but it doesn't make up for the higher salaries of coal jobs. Moreover, subsidized or free re-training for entire coal communities may be needed
(Fossil fuel) If I buy an electric vehicle, I won't be able to drive it wherever I want without worrying about running out of energy	(Renewables) The average American drives less than 36 miles/day, and with most EV's getting over 150 miles/charge, it's usually a non-factor. Range anxiety is definitely real, but can be managed by planning ahead
(Renewables) Don't you care about having a clean earth and having healthy jobs?	(Fossil fuel) Of course! Everyone cares about those things. But the reason this industry is important to me is…

Section 3:
Communication Tools

The Importance of Allyship

Conversations with people who have opposing viewpoints is difficult to begin with, and it can be even more of a challenge if the other person doesn't look, talk, or think like you. It can be downright hard when people have already set out to blame someone else for their problems, economic uncertainty or public health risk.

In previous chapters you likely identified as one "side" or the other, but in this chapter, we want to take a different approach. We want to highlight that bridging the gap is not always about you – sometimes it is about supporting others. This can be representing a voice that is left out, inviting people to have a seat at the table, or sticking up for others on their behalf. This is called *allyship* and it's an important component of working towards finding common ground.

For example, in the realm of diversity, equity and inclusion (DEI), conversations can very quickly devolve into an "us vs. them" mentality. Even the most well-intentioned conversations can go off the rails when someone insults or discriminates against someone else.

A recent example of this occurred when many Americans, including the President, began calling the Coronavirus the "China virus" or the "Wuhan virus." This inevitably pinned blame on Asians and Asian Americans who were further discriminated against as a result, with many businesses suffering economic losses and several individuals being physically assaulted. The World Health Organization discourages naming viruses after specific places, people, animals or food for this very reason – to avoid the negative consequences that result for that group.

Being an ally means speaking up when these type of discriminatory statements are made. It also means that you make sure that multiple perspectives are taken into account and that people are involved in meetings, conversations and decisions even if you aren't of the same race, gender, ethnicity, sexual orientation, etc. as they are.

We have highlighted four areas of focus to becoming a better ally and helping find common ground:

- Understand

- Listen

- Empathize

- Reflect

This chapter is not all-encompassing of every opinion or layer of this topic – it simply aims to bring attention to allyship as an important factor in productively talking to the "other side." You may not have considered what it is like to walk in the shoes of marginalized communities, and that is why it is important to bring in these voices as a component of those interactions.

The authors acknowledge that this chapter is written from their perspectives and inherently stems from their own identities, biases and experiences.

1) Understand

One of the reasons we include DEI as a case study is because there are inherent privileges and societal norms that need changing in how we relate and interact with one another. While one can't experience every DEI perspective, everyone can be an ally.

DEI is about empowering everyone to be given the same chance. As President Kennedy was fond of saying, a rising tide lifts all boats. One of the reasons it has become a flashpoint issue is that the media and politicians have propagated the idea that societal success comes in the form of a single pie. This leads to a misplaced belief that if you provide opportunity for one group, it will decrease everyone else's opportunity. People are afraid that someone else will take their slice of the pie.

This is a sticking point because typically a person's fears stem from a concern of missing out or having an opportunity taken from them.

This false narrative has been played out for generations and needs to be corrected and addressed head on.

This is where allyship can be critical in demonstrating to others that it is possible to support others while achieving the same level of opportunity for oneself.

Getting our terms clear

When you ask someone to describe DEI, you are likely to get a different response from every single person you talk to. Therefore, to ensure all readers start on the same page (pun intended), let's use the following definitions for this chapter:

Diversity: All the ways in which people differ.

Diversity refers to race, ethnicity, gender, age, sexual orientation, national origin, religion, disability, socioeconomic status, education, marital status, language, and physical appearance. It also may include diversity of thought as well, because while one person can fall under the same physical identities, their ideas, perspectives and values differ.

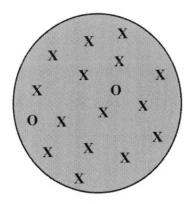 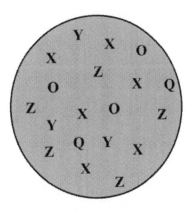

In a group with low diversity, the few who stand out are often treated as different or as the "other." In the left visual, your eyes go straight to the O's. In the right image, however, your eye doesn't see any pattern. When diversity exists, it is easier to see and feel equal.

Equity: The fair treatment, access, opportunity, and advancement for all people, while striving to eliminate barriers that have prevented the full participation of some groups.

Equality means that everyone starts from the same place. This is good, but some still face bigger obstacles than others. Equity, on the other hand, starts everyone the same distance away from the goal, no matter their original circumstances. This is why you'd want to strive for *equity* instead of equality.

The next visual demonstrates this difference by comparing three people who are facing obstacles, and because of where they start and how much they have to overcome, they all have distinctly different experiences.

Inclusion: The act of creating environments in which any individual or group can be and feel welcomed, supported, and valued to fully participate.

While an inclusive group is diverse by definition, a diverse group isn't always inclusive. This means that it is not only about getting a seat at the proverbial table, but also being valued and listened to as much as anyone else. The two examples below show the difference.

Diverse	Diverse & Inclusive
AAAABBBBCCCCDDDD	ACBDCADDBCADCBAB
In the example above, there are four different letters. However, the letters are all grouped together. Though it may be diverse, each letter sticks to the ones most like themselves. This happens a lot when people sub-group with people who are more like them.	This graphic shows both a diverse and inclusive group. The four different letters are equal and mixed throughout. If the letters represent people, they are interacting with others from different identities and each letter is included.

DEI is a win-win in business

When talking to the "other side" about DEI, be sure to highlight the benefits. Studies have shown that the more diverse a group is, the more resilient and the better performing a group is, no matter the size. Two studies published in the Harvard Business Review backed this up, demonstrating that diversity in fact increases innovation, revenue and greater profits. And a 2016 study of over 20,000 firms in 91 countries found that "companies with more female executives were more profitable."[77]

Showing intentionality, striving for diversity and engaging multiple stakeholders often takes more time and runs counter to many executives' desire to act quickly, but it is worth it.

I've witnessed numerous times professionally where decision makers were so focused on "getting something done and fast" that they sacrificed diversity and inclusion for speed. Then, once the proposed policy or business idea was put into place, it ran into all types of barriers and ended up failing. These barriers could have been avoided if the various voices of community stakeholders were heard and incorporated on the front end. In fact, studies show that while diversity, equity and inclusion efforts do take longer, their solutions typically have a greater chance of success over the long run.[78]

Demonstrating this higher success rate that diverse teams provide is a great tool for allies in advocating for DEI initiatives. If your company is trying to rush into a project without full stakeholder engagement, show your leadership those statistics and stop them! Making sure everyone is invited to the table not only brings in new ideas, but also just makes good business sense.

And once you get the leadership on board, then it's easier to make larger shifts towards equity. A good friend of mine, Kim Vu has experienced that "we can only fix the institutional things if and when the top of the organization commits to doing their own work." Thus, appealing to those in power can be significant in creating change.

2) Listen

If you are asking someone about their opinion on a controversial topic, or if someone is challenging your position, listen with the intent of truly grasping what they are saying and why. Instead of mentally preparing your next point or counterpoint, listen to learn a new perspective on the issue. People have different life experiences and as was said earlier, while you can disagree with their opinion, you cannot disagree with their experience.

Feeling like one's voice isn't being heard or respected is a huge area of dissatisfaction, especially for women, minorities and working-class folks who feel that way regularly. Remember that to find common ground, those in power need to consider what actions they could change personally that address these areas of concern. For specific examples, read on for the "8 Recommendations for Being an Ally" later in this chapter.

DEI conversations can be difficult to bring up, but if we are to make a cultural shift towards equity for all, then we need to normalize tough conversation topics like these. Vu continues, "Let's normalize these conversations, as normal as any conversation about our business operations, marketing or financial performance."

The exception to this, of course, is if someone is using certain speech that is hateful, demeaning or harmful. In those cases, it is perfectly acceptable and important to speak up, challenge them or even walk away.

3) Empathize

Empathy enables you to better understand the "other side" as it helps to visualize spending a day in the other person's shoes. You'd be amazed at how your perspective can change almost immediately, when you do this from a point of empathy.

when I'm older

If I do the same job as a boy, I want to be paid just as much. That's all

For example, I'm pretty comfortable and confident here in the US, but if you drop me off in the middle of Beijing, the same cannot be said. I will struggle with the most basic things like ordering a meal, asking where the bathroom is or finding my way around. In China, I'm illiterate. I cannot even speak basic Mandarin or read street signs. So, to the average Beijinger, I probably don't seem very intelligent. Moreover, I already stick out in an uncomfortable manner because of my race, ethnicity, hair color and even height!

I share this anecdote because almost everyone has a moment in their life when they felt like the odd person out. I've found that using a personal example and humor can help someone from the "other side" gain perspective. It provides an opening to discuss how it may feel for women, minorities or working-class folks in their everyday experience.

Natalie has a story as well, of stepping into the shoes of having a physical disability. As a long-time water polo player, Natalie developed lasting lung issues from breathing too much heavily-chlorinated air. Though she struggled in the pool, this didn't affect her day-to-day life too much at the time.

However, this disability became a major issue for her when the Coronavirus hit – because of the damage it can do to the lungs. On the surface, Natalie seems like she would be the least susceptible person to the virus because she is an active and healthy young person. At first, this led people to act careless around her.

At the onset of the pandemic, she felt pressured to continue socializing and going out to bars by other young people who didn't see themselves as being in any real danger. No one thought she might be either, because of the assumptions that they made about her health. As a result, she had to either put her health at risk or feel guilty or embarrassed for staying home.

This was a time where Natalie really needed allies, and she benefited greatly from her closest friends who stepped up and spoke for her so that she wouldn't have to always feel uncomfortable saying no.

For many of you reading this, Allyship manifested itself during COVID-19 in many ways including:

- Legitimizing and appreciating people who were taking action by staying home, whether they were vulnerable or simply trying to avoid becoming a carrier

- Supporting the decisions of people who were showing high levels of concern and social distancing, rather than looking down on them as "overreacting"

- Checking in with loved ones and the most vulnerable, who may not have seemed like they were having a hard time on the surface, but were often struggling physically, mentally, emotionally and/or financially

As you can imagine, having allies makes hard times much, much more manageable. This is not only the case in a crisis, but for all identity groups and all the time. Thinking from the perspective of others and making an effort to empathize with them goes a long way.

4) Reflect

Think about your own identities and ask yourself what it would be like if things were different. Reflect on what answers you come up with. For each identity listed below, we have provided a simple question to stimulate your thoughts on some of the daily challenges that people face who are different from you. I don't pretend to cover every issue because each group has incredible depth, so I invite you to explore more resources on understanding the dynamics of each if you are so inclined. This is just a list of starter questions for each of us to consider and check our own privilege.

- **Race:** How might you feel if your personality, values and identity were constantly predetermined based on what you look like or on preconceived notions about "people like you?"

- **Ethnicity:** Have you ever been asked, "Where are you from?" by someone who, despite the fact that you were born and raised in the US, is just interested in the country of your non-white ethnicity?

- **Gender:** How might your life at work, home and with your friends be different if you were the opposite sex, transgender or gender fluid? Have you ever felt judged by simply introducing yourself or your partner by your personal pronouns (or similarly, introduced yourself incorrectly just to avoid making the other person uncomfortable)?

- **LGBTQ+:** Have you ever felt uncomfortable simply introducing yourself or your partner because of your sexual orientation?

- **Culture:** Have you been looked down upon as "weird" or "unnatural" for practicing very normal cultural customs, like dressing/eating a certain way or celebrating a holiday?

- **Age:** Have you ever been not taken seriously because of your age or how old you look? How did this make you feel?

- **Language:** Has your social and dating life or ability to land a job been affected by a language barrier? How might this impact peoples' perception of you?

- **Class:** Have you felt frustratingly left out of the conversation simply based on your income or socioeconomic class?

- **Veteran status:** Have you had an experience so impactful that few others are able to understand or relate to it?

- **Physical disability:** Have you ever considered how different your daily routine, job or lifestyle would be if you were unable to see, speak, hear, move, or had chronic pain?

- **Mental disability:** Have you struggled to perform day-to-day activities? How has mental illness affected a friend or loved one of yours, and in what ways?

8 Recommendations to Being an Effective Ally

1) **SPEAK UP:** make sure those not at the table are included

2) **STEP BACK:** allow those to step forward who don't often have a chance to speak or lead

3) **MAKE INTENTIONAL CHANGES:** quit defaulting to what's easiest, embrace the difficult

4) **ASK QUESTIONS:** especially to people in power – for example, women shouldn't always have to be the ones who bring up gender pay equity

5) **ASSUME GOOD INTENTIONS:** regardless of presentation

6) **ACKNOWLEDGE:** certain identities hold privilege or are disadvantaged in society

7) **BE COMFORTABLE:** it's okay to not know every aspect of an issue or a perspective – welcome it and learn

8) **CREATE SPACE:** sometimes you can be an ally just by holding the space in which these conversations can happen

Summary

Allyship is an essential component of creating the space needed to find common ground. It is critical to advancing diversity, equity, and inclusion in society, and everyone can be a better ally.

If we are going to solve our largest socio-economic, public health and environmental challenges, these conversations need to become more frequent, normal and comfortable. We all need to self-reflect, listen, empathize more and learn.

We need to level the playing field for all people and sometimes act as an ambassador for finding common ground. This takes the form of being an ally, and to do so, we must:

- Learn how to host, facilitate and start difficult conversations on race, gender, class, sexual orientation, disability, age, ethnicity, culture and more

- Become comfortable having these conversations to normalize them

- Realize that as an ally, sometimes it is your job to speak up, and other times it is time to step aside and allow space for others to speak and lead

- Understand and clearly communicate the benefits and needs of being more diverse, equitable, and inclusive

- Personalize the conversation by using your own experiences when having a difficult conversation

- Know you may have to put yourself out there to be an ally, but that it is worth it

- Stand up for others not represented in the room and speak up for them, and with them, so that they aren't always the ones who have to do so

Difficult Conversations 101

Learning how to engage with someone who disagrees with you and finding common ground is hard work. Think for a second what your gut reaction is to the crowd cheering at a political rally for the other candidate. Or to someone who is calling the Coronavirus a hoax while you are worried about getting sick? Or put yourselves into the shoes of the person who is pressing their religion on to you?

They probably care and believe as deeply in their values as you do your own, but more often than not, our knee jerk reaction is to get angry and dismiss that person's ideas. Engaging in a difficult conversation is tough, can be uncomfortable and often takes patience, empathy and (at times) suspending your own beliefs to truly understand where the person is coming from.

This chapter highlights practical techniques I've used both personally and professionally to lower the temperature during difficult and sometimes disagreeable conversations. The hope is that with the following 10 steps, you can find greater success and common ground.

1. CONNECT ON A PERSONAL LEVEL

2. LISTEN BEFORE BEING HEARD

3. LOWER THE TEMPERATURE THROUGH EMPATHY

4. IT'S NOT WHAT YOU SAY, IT'S HOW YOU SAY IT

5. NEVER SAY "YOU" OR "YOU PEOPLE"

6. ACCEPT DIFFERENT STYLES

7. DON'T CORRECT THE SMALL STUFF

8. DISAGREE RESPECTFULLY

9. DON'T TRY TO IMPRESS WITH BIG WORDS

10. DON'T ASSUME

"I have learned that when trying to influence someone's thinking, I should approach it not as an argument I am trying to win but instead as a conversation that I am trying to start."

– Dave Phemister, Kentucky State Director at The Nature Conservancy[79]

Step 1: Connect on a personal level

As mentioned in the Finding Common Ground chapter, the first step is connecting on a human and personal level. We all learned in elementary school to follow the Golden Rule and treat people the way you'd like to be treated. While this may seem like an oversimplification, it isn't.

When I enter a meeting, I try to get to know the people in the room first: where they are from, what they do, if they are a sports fan, etc. People are more responsive and respectful if you first have a connection.

KoAnn Skrzyniarz of Sustainable Brands adds that "the notion of acknowledging our shared humanity and creating a safe place for dialogue is pretty important when trying to have a productive conversation." In addition to this, she pointed out, you need to come to the conversation humble. You have to be vulnerable first if you want others to be vulnerable to you.[80]

Connect, find commonalities, build rapport and respect. That is the first step.

Step 2: Listen before being heard

If you want to be heard, start by listening first. Sounds painfully simple, but sometimes we need to "shut up and listen."[81] Understand before trying to be understood.

This is a hard skill to master, especially if you believe the other person is predisposed to disagree with you. It means that when you are chomping at the bit to make your point, you need to check yourself and zip those lips. You already know what you want to say, but you need to know the other person's perspective – what THEY care about, and why. This is not only important in making sure the other person feels heard, but it also provides you with a better idea for how to tailor the conversation and determine the points you want to make.

When trying to have a conversation with someone on something you likely disagree with, use the following five questions to help get a truer sense as to what is behind their beliefs.

5 questions to ask yourself while listening:

- What are the two most important things to this person?

- Why are they so important to them?

- What is the true anxiety behind their frustration?

- What is their ideal outcome?

- How can we help them reach their goal?

I liken it to being in a relationship. I'm sure many of you can relate. When your significant other gets angry or blows their top over something seemingly insignificant like where you left a dirty dish, then it's probably not really about the dishes. More often than not, it's about bigger issues in your relationship and the dishes were just what set off the argument. Often there is feeling *behind* what is being said, so you need to peel back that onion first.

When you listen from this perspective, as opposed to your own, you can better understand their reasoning and then work to unlock win-win strategies. Bruce McGlenn says that, "Once we see things from a different perspective in one area, maybe it's easier to do so in other areas as well."[82]

Step 3: Lower the temperature through empathy

Effective listening requires empathy. Have you ever been in a situation where someone is so frustrated that nobody is listening to them, that they start screaming and yelling?

The most effective way to lower the volume and temperature of the conversation is to empathize. Put yourself in their shoes of frustration. Acknowledge them with eye contact, nodding and provide verbal and non-verbal affirmations. When someone is that worked up, they want you to feel what they feel. You can't have a productive conversation with this person until they calm down. When you empathize, you can begin to understand. Don't try to listen with the idea that you already have the solution. Instead, honor their personal experience, be compassionate and truly hear them. Ask yourself how you'd feel if this happened to you?

Step 4: Realize it may not be *what* you say, but *how* you say it

Have you ever been in a conversation while someone is doing what I call the "Manhattan Lookover"? This means that while you're speaking, they are looking around to see if there is someone else that they should be talking to. Or, have you ever tried to talk to someone who is staring down at their phone the whole time? How did this make you feel? The person may in fact be listening to you, but you probably don't feel that they are paying attention or giving you the respect that you deserve.

Body language and tone can matter just as much in a conversation as the point you are making. If you address someone in a respectful tone, make eye contact, and speak at a reasonable volume; people tend to hear you more accurately and feel better about responding. However, if your tone is off and you are showing irritation or anger, that emotion is what people will focus on. If that happens, your point is lost before it can even be made.

Step 5: Never say "You" or "You People"

Never use the word "you." That hits people at their core, makes it personal and immediately puts them on the defensive. Remember, you are disagreeing with their statements, not attacking them personally. The words you use will make a difference in how they will respond. Disagree with the idea, point, argument, policy, rule, or whatever, but don't make it personal.

See if you notice the difference:

- You are trying to kill my business

- The regulations and taxes that are being proposed will kill my business

The first one makes it personal. The second one addresses the idea, rather than the individual. There is a huge difference in how the other person will take it if it doesn't embarrass them or feel like an attack. Talking about the statement and the specific idea allows both sides to have a conversation as opposed to a heated and hurtful argument. Natasha Lamb says, "You can appeal to people's better angels when not embarrassing them."[83]

Step 6: Acknowledge different learning and communication styles

One of the traps that most people fall into is that they think everyone is just like them. They believe that people listen and learn the way they do. The reality is that everyone processes information and handles interactions very differently.

In fact, there are five different learning styles. When trying to talk to someone from the "other side," you need to realize that *how* you deliver this information may be as important as what you are trying to say.

Learner Types:

	Optimal Environment	**Ineffective Environment**
Auditory	• Listening to explanations • Reciting information out loud	• Noises might distract, resulting in a need for a quiet place
Visual	• Looking at graphics, reading or watching a demonstration	• Listening to a long explanation
Hands-on (Touch/Physical)	• "Hands-on" experiences, writing and taking notes	• Sitting still
Verbal	• Dialogue (listening, speaking and repeating) • Using words (writing, speech)	• Working independently • Sitting quietly to think things through
Logical (Reasoning)	• Asking questions and investigating • Solving problems	• Being asked to do something without knowing the context or having the ability to ask questions

For example, if you are trying to communicate with someone who is a visual learner, but you only use speech to convey your message, your idea won't sink in as well because they need to see it.

Some questions you might consider asking yourself during your conversation include: are they extroverted and processing out loud, or are they introverted and holding off on speaking until they organize the entirety of their thoughts? Could they be an experiential learner that needs to learn by doing?

It's impossible to know this going into every conversation, but if you pay attention to these style differences, you'll be able to craft your message more appropriately to the person you are talking to and to a wider variety of audiences.

Step 7: Don't correct the small stuff

Have you ever been telling a story and someone stops you to correct a fact or your grammar? This is super annoying and interrupts your thought process. There may be times when someone is making a point and you feel the sudden urge to clarify a date, fact or piece of grammar – DON'T. What's important is that you understand what they are trying to communicate, not that they are grammatically accurate.

For example, I grew up in a family where five of the six of us have been teachers at one point in our lives. Yes, my brother Brett was the outlier.

I can't tell you how many times as a kid when I was trying to tell a story and a member of my family stopped me to correct my grammar. This was so annoying that my default was to just disengage and stop telling my story, no matter how important I felt it was. Focusing on the small stuff is a sign that you are *not* acknowledging the bigger point of someone's story.

Step 8: Disagree respectfully

It can be hard to keep your cool when the person you are talking to is someone whose beliefs and values may be 180° opposite of your own. Remember, being respectful doesn't mean you have to compromise your own values. Be sure to be authentic, maintain your integrity and be cool, calm and collected.

If you find yourself in a heated argument, rationality often goes out the window and it's easy to retreat to raw emotion. When this happens, people often stop listening and just focus on trying to "win" the argument by saying the most hurtful thing.

Sandra Richard, Host at Camp St. Malo, Chapel on the Rock shares her insight on this. "I realized that I was looking at a certain individual as being my *adversary*. When I made a mental decision to change the way I saw them, it made a world of difference. And while nothing about them has changed, we have a great relationship now." She advises that while disagreeing with someone, we must regard them as another reasoning person with dignity.[84]

Therefore, show respect and acknowledge the points they make by saying something like, "That's a new perspective for me, I hadn't thought about it that way. You've given me something to think about." This is in your best interest because by acknowledging them, they are more likely to return the favor.

Sometimes, the easiest way to do this is to pay a compliment. Say something like "I can see how dedicated and passionate you are about this issue, and I commend you." Show the opposition the same level of respect that you receive from people who share your point of view. This is a way to remain authentic to your beliefs and still be respectful at the same time. I've found that paying a compliment, and then shifting the conversation ever so slightly towards the middle, can lead to a significant breakthrough in communicating with people. There are often more than one or two ways to accomplish something, and communication is no exception.

Know when to give up, though

Recognize that if the person is disrespectful, using vulgar language or is unwilling to listen to you, sometimes you just have to punt and walk away.

Step 9: Don't try and impress with big words

Simplify and put things in layperson's terms. There is nothing more off-putting than when you are trying to have a conversation and you don't even understand the words coming out of the other person's mouth. You can't find common ground with someone if they can't comprehend what you are saying. Use language, words and examples they can relate to or are familiar with.

For example, about 10 years ago, I was serving on the Board of the Center for Ethical Leadership. During a presentation at the Board retreat, one of the staffers was using words that none of us had ever heard before. In this staffer's desire to impress us with big words, she totally lost us instead. Therefore, when you are trying to find common ground, be sure to keep the conversation in layperson's terms.

Step 10: When you assume, you make an ASS out of U and ME

I know you've heard this phrase before, but it holds true. Too often people assume things about another person but in reality, we have no idea what is going on in that other person's life or what experiences are behind their beliefs. Don't make assumptions. When you do this, you miss a key opportunity to level set, understand where that person truly is coming from and form a relationship.

I remember trying to convince a Chief Financial Officer that his company should take sustainability more seriously. So, when we met for coffee, I launched into all the business and financial reasons his company should move forward – assuming that because he was a finance person, all he cared about was money. He responded "No, I totally get it, what I'm concerned about is how to actually engage my employees." I had made the mistake of spending 20 minutes talking about something that he already knew, and not a second on what his main concern was.

"When talking to someone from what you might assume as the 'other side,' ask yourself 'what do they value?' That entry point is typically much richer than any assumption you may have made."

– Ben Packard, Executive Director at University of Washington EarthLab[85]

Summary

While you may not be able to change the minds of someone on the "other side" right away, you now have 10 specific skills to help you start the conversation and begin bridge-building. Be conscious of how you engage and be sure to:

- Connect on a personal level

- Listen before being heard

- Lower the tone and temperature of the conversation through empathy

- Show that you are interested in what they have to say

- Use words that don't put people on the defensive (e.g. "you people")

- Realize that everyone communicates differently (introverts and extroverts)

- Hear their point and do not get hung up on grammar or specific names/dates

- Disagree with respect

- Speak in the language they are using

- Never assume something about the other person

Conclusion

Talking to the "other side" is easier than we think, especially once we get past our preconceived notions and emotions. You'll find that there are opportunities to find common ground all around us, and during these turbulent times we need to double our efforts to do just that – whether it be about public health, the economy, climate change or whatever.

If we are going to effectively make change, it is essential that we respect and listen to others. We need to seek to understand, empathize and authentically listen to people's hopes, dreams, anxieties and fears, so that can we truly uncover what is at the core of their beliefs and identify win-win solutions.

Remember, there is more that unites us than divides us. As we laid out in chapter after chapter, all humans seek the same basic things and what typically trips us up are the means to achieving those ends. The "other side" is in quotes throughout this book, because in reality, there is no "other side." We are all in this together.

By refocusing our energies towards our shared aspirations and being willing to compromise – as opposed to only seeing our perceived and real differences – we can return to a time of civility and getting things done. Sandra Richard reminds, "Don't look at people like they are an adversary – if you can make this mental shift, everything changes."[86]

In writing this book, we openly acknowledge that we didn't get to every controversial point or issue, especially while writing at such a fluid time of uncertainty. Our hope is that the tools, techniques, case studies and messages found throughout these pages will help us all change the tone and tenor of these conversations and enable us to do the work that must get done.

Bridging these divides isn't going to happen overnight. We need all of us, and I mean all, to make a concerted effort to be those catalysts for change. The stakes are too high. We can and we must do this!

How to Start a Difficult Conversation in One Page

Do you struggle with talking to people you disagree with?
Follow these helpful tips!

EMOTIONAL CONFLICTS
Where have you had difficult conversations? Why do you think that is the case?

GETTING TO THE CORE OF THE ARGUMENT: ASK THE 5 W's
1. What does this person care about?
2. Why do they care about this?
3. Where do their fears and anxieties come from?
4. What aspirations do they have for the outcome of their idea?
5. What can you do to help them get there?

TIP: Ask yourself the 5 W's, too. You might be surprised about the root of your opinions! There might be some overlap at the fundamental level with the person you are trying to talk to.

TIP: Focus on what they are saying, not how they are saying it. People can get fired up about issues that they care about – their voices may raise, and emotions might take over. Acknowledge them and listen calmly.

POTENTIAL COMMONALITIES
Remember, you likely have a lot in common! These could be great ways of getting the conversation started. Do any of the following apply to both of you?

☐ Has a pet at home   ☐ Started new hobby during COVID-19
☐ Is a football fan   ☐ Can't seem to keep plants alive
☐ Dips fries in your shake   ☐ Take too many photos of your child
☐ Was in a fraternity/sorority   ☐ Likes The Beatles
☐ Other (please specify) _____

SOCIAL INDICATORS
Are you currently using any of the following while trying to have these conversations? Check all that apply and pay special attention to the boxes left unchecked. That's where you need to improve!

☐ Empathy   ☐ Patience   ☐ Positive/Simple Language
☐ Respect   ☐ Active Listening   ☐ Personal Experiences

References

[1] James N. Druckman, Matthew S. Levendusky, and Audrey McLain, "No Need to Watch: How the Effects of Partisan Media Can Spread via Interpersonal Discussions," *American Journal of Political Science*, 2017.

[2] Lee De-Wit, Cameron Brick, and Sander Van Der Linden, "Are Social Media Driving Political Polarization?," Greater Good Science Center at UC Berkeley, January 16, 2019.

[3] Tim Moore, phone interview, September 23, 2019.

[4] Stephen Hawkins et al., "Hidden Tribes: A Study of America's Polarized Landscape," August 21, 2019.

[5] KoAnn Vikoren Skrzyniarz, phone interview, September 10, 2019.

[6] Peter Fenn, phone interview, September 4, 2019.

[7] "Political Polarization in the American Public," *Pew Research Center's U.S. Politics & Policy* (blog), June 12, 2014.

[8] "Nature, Nurture And Your Politics," *Hidden Brain* (NPR, October 8, 2018); Steve Smith, "Study Suggests Biological Truths to Political Stereotypes," University of Nebraska-Lincoln, n.d.

[9] Benji Backer, phone interview, October 3, 2019.

[10] Josh Chaitin, phone interview, November 7, 2019.

[11] Webster, interview.

[12] Skrzyniarz, interview.

[13] Natasha Lamb, video interview, October 18, 2019.

[14] Bruce McGlenn, phone interview, September 9, 2019.

[15] Skrzyniarz, interview.

[16] Fenn, interview.

[17] Kim Parker et al., "What Unites and Divides Urban, Suburban and Rural Communities," Pew Research Center's Social & Demographic Trends Project, May 22, 2018.

[18] Kim Parker et al., "How People in Urban, Suburban and Rural Communities See Each Other – and Say Others See Them," Pew Research Center's Social & Demographic Trends Project, May 22, 2018.

[19] Bruce Franklin McGlenn, "To Shoot, or Not to Shoot...," *Human Nature Hunting School* (blog), November 20, 1999.

[20] Dean Lueck, "An Economic Guide to State Wildlife Management" (PERC, n.d.).

[21] Kim Parker et al., "Views of Problems Facing Urban, Suburban and Rural Communities," Pew Research Center's Social & Demographic Trends Project, May 22, 2018.

[22] "A Landowner's Guide To Preventing Big Game Damage and Filing Damage Claims" (Idaho Fish & Game, 2018).

[23] Todd Myers, phone interview, August 27, 2019.

[24] Dave Phemister, phone interview, September 11, 2019.

[25] "Free the Green," The Nature Conservancy, n.d.; Carol Labashosky, "Removal of Lock and Dam 6 Completed on Green River, Kentucky," www.army.mil, n.d.

[26] Mark Muro, Jacob Whiton, and Robert Maxim, "How China's Proposed Tariffs Could Affect U.S. Workers and Industries," *Brookings* (blog), April 9, 2018.

[27] "Wind Energy Factsheet," University of Michigan Center for Sustainable Systems, n.d.

[28] "Crop Values 2018 Summary" (USDA, April 2019).

[29] "Wind Power Pays $222 Million A Year To Rural Landowners," American Wind Energy Association, March 22, 2016.

[30] "May Ranch Avoided Grassland Conversion Project," *Native Energy* (blog), 2018.

[31] Sid Yadav, "May Ranch Grasslands Protection," Cool Effect, n.d.; OAR US EPA, "Greenhouse Gas Equivalencies Calculator," Data and Tools, US EPA, n.d.

[32] "Know Your Farmer/Rancher, Know Your Carbon Offsets," *Pinhead Institute: A Smithsonian Affiliate* (blog), n.d.

[33] "UN Global Compact-Accenture Strategy 2019 CEO Study – The Decade to Deliver: A Call to Business Action" (United Nations Global Compact, 2019).

[34] Phemister, interview.

[35] "S&P 500 Environmental & Socially Responsible Index," S&P Dow Jones Indices, n.d.

[36] "S&P 500," S&P Dow Jones Indices, n.d.

[37] "Dow Jones Sustainability U.S. Composite Index (USD)," S&P Dow Jones Indices, n.d.

[38] "Dow Jones Industrial Average," S&P Dow Jones Indices, n.d.

[39] "Private Equity and Responsible Investment: An Opportunity for Value Creation" (World Wildlife Fund, Doughty Hanson, n.d.).

[40] "Carbon Disclosure Project (CDP)," n.d.

[41] Letitia Webster, phone interview, August 28, 2019.

[42] Patrick Drum, phone interview, August 22, 2019.

[43] Matthew E Kahn et al., "Long-Term Macroeconomic Effects of Climate Change: A Cross-Country Analysis," Working Paper (National Bureau of Economic Research, August 2019).

[44] "Culture Next Global Trends Report" (Spotify For Brands, 2019).

[45] Julie Hootkin and Tanya Meck, "Call to Action in the Age of Trump, Business & Politics: Do They Mix?" (Global Strategy Group, 2018).

[46] "BC's Carbon Tax Shift After Five Years," Smart Prosperity Institute (Formerly Sustainable Prosperity), n.d.

[47] "British Columbia's Carbon Tax," Government of B.C., n.d.

[48] Brian Blankespoor, Susmita Dasgupta, and Glenn-Marie Lange, "Mangroves as a Protection from Storm Surges in a Changing Climate," *Ambio*, October 27, 2016.

[49] Jodie Berezin, Samantha Gray, and James Woodward, "Using Mangroves to Mitigate Hurricane Damage to the Southern US Coast," Debating Science, University of Massachusetts Amherst, April 24, 2018.

[50] "Lower Duwamish River," Damage Assessment, Remediation, and Restoration Program (DARRP), July 18, 2019.

[51] "Habitat Restoration along the Lower Duwamish Waterway" (Port of Seattle, City of Seattle, King County, Boeing, n.d.).

[52] Cary Funk and Meg Hefferon, "Millennial and Gen Z Republicans Stand out from Their Elders on Climate and Energy Issues," *Pew Research Center* (blog), November 25, 2019.

[53] "The Harris Poll," The Harris Poll, n.d.

[54] "On Climate Change, Younger Republicans Now Sound like Democrats," Resilience, September 16, 2019.

[55] Backer, interview.

[56] Adam B. Smith, "2018's Billion Dollar Disasters in Context," NOAA Climate.gov, February 7, 2019.

[57] "Effects of a Changing Climate to the Department of Defense" (US Department of Defense, January 2019).

[58] Paul E. Roege, "Creating Value Through Resilience" (International Risk Governance Council (IRGC), n.d.).

[59] Weimer Pursell, "Powers of Persuasion: Poster Art from World War II," National Archives, Office of Price Administration, 1943.

[60] "Sustain the Mission Project: Casualty Factors for Fuel and Water Resupply Convoys," Final Technical Report (Army Environmental Policy Institute, September 2009); "Powering the Future Force: New Power & Energy Technologies for the Warfighter" (Defense Technical Information Center, n.d.).

[61] Rita Boland, "Marines Test Alternative Power in Afghanistan," SIGNAL Magazine, March 2011; Justin Gerdes, "Marines Push to Front Lines in Renewable Energy Innovation," Yale Environment 360, June 27, 2013.

[62] Bill Chappell, "Solar-Powered Marines See Gains In Afghanistan," National Public Radio (NPR), January 17, 2011.

[63] *Force Multiplying Technologies for Logistics Support to Military Operations* (Washington, D.C.: The National Academies Press, 2014).

[64] Sam LaGrone, "Navy Set to Install Hybrid Electric Drives in Destroyer Fleet Starting Next Year," America's Navy, 2014; Timothy Gardner, "U.S. Military Marches Forward on Green Energy, despite Trump," *Reuters*, February 28, 2017.

[65] John C. Stennis, "The Great Green Fleet Explained," America's Navy, June 27, 2016.

[66] "Army Awards 20 Additional Contracts for Renewable Energy Technologies," US Office of Energy Efficiency & Renewable Energy, February 26, 2014; "Energy Flight Plan" (U.S. Air Force, 2017); "Renewable Energy Projects," U.S. Navy

Energy, Environment and Climate Change, October 2012; "United States Marine Corps Expeditionary Energy Strategy and Implementation Plan" (US Marine Corps, 2011).

[67] Moshe Schwartz, Katherine Blakeley, and Ronald O'Rourke, "Department of Defense Energy Initiatives: Background and Issues for Congress" (Congressional Research Service, December 10, 2012).

[68] David Vergun, "Soldiers Using Sunlight to Improve Combat Capability," U.S. Army, November 14, 2012.

[69] "U.S. Electricity Generation from Renewables Surpassed Coal in April," U.S. Energy Information Administration (EIA), June 26, 2019; "Natural Gas Prices in 2016 Were the Lowest in Nearly 20 Years - Today in Energy - U.S. Energy Information Administration (EIA)," U.S. Energy Information Administration (EIA), January 13, 2017.

[70] "Renewable Electricity Levelized Cost Of Energy Already Cheaper Than Fossil Fuels, And Prices Keep Plunging," Energy Innovation: Policy & Technology LLC, January 22, 2018; Dan Gearino, "New Wind and Solar Power Is Cheaper Than Existing Coal in Much of the U.S., Analysis Finds," Inside Climate News, March 25, 2019.

[71] "U.S. Energy and Employment Report" (US Department of Energy, January 2017).

[72] "Northern Spotted Owl," U.S. Fish & Wilflife Service, January 8, 2020; "Advanced Wood Product Manufacturing Study for Cross-Laminated Timber Acceleration in Oregon & SW Washington" (Pacific Northwest Manufacturing Partnership, 2017).

[73] "Logging Workers: Occupational Outlook Handbook," U.S. Bureau of Labor Statistics, n.d.

[74] Kristen Kleiman, "Low Carbon Policies Create Jobs and Spur a Healthy Economy," The Climate Trust, March 20, 2017.

[75] "Fastest Growing Occupations," U.S. Bureau of Labor Statistics, September 4, 2019.

[76] "American FactFinder," U.S. Census Bureau, July 1, 2019.

[77] David Rock, Heidi Grant, and Jacqui Grey, "Diverse Teams Feel Less Comfortable — and That's Why They Perform Better," *Harvard Business Review*, September 22, 2016.

[78] "Why Diversity and Inclusion Matter: Quick Take," Catalyst, August 1, 2018.

[79] Phemister, interview.

[80] Skrzyniarz, interview.

[81] Ben Packard, phone interview, September 4, 2019.

[82] McGlenn, interview.

[83] Lamb, interview.

[84] Sandra Richard, In-person interview, January 10, 2020.

[85] Packard, interview.

[86] Richard, interview.

Made in the USA
Middletown, DE
22 January 2021

32178985R00080